# Hairdressing Business Management

# HAIRDRESSING
## BUSINESS MANAGEMENT

**Annette Mieske**

OXFORD
BSP PROFESSIONAL BOOKS
LONDON EDINBURGH BOSTON
MELBOURNE PARIS BERLIN VIENNA

First published 1990

British Library
Cataloging in Publication Data
Mieske, Annette
   Hairdressing business management.
   1. Hairdressing services. Organisation
   I. Title
   646.7242068

ISBN 0-632-02592-1

BSP Professional Books
A division of Blackwell Scientific
   Publications Ltd
Editorial Offices:
Osney Mead, Oxford OX2 0EL
   (Orders: Tel. 0865 240201)
25 John Street, London WC1N 2BL
23 Ainslie Place, Edinburgh EH3 6AJ
3 Cambridge Center, Suite 208, Cambridge
   MA 02142, USA
54 University Street, Carlton, Victoria 3053,
   Australia

Set by DP Photosetting, Aylesbury, Bucks
Printed and bound in Great Britain by
the University Press, Cambridge

For my parents and daughter Kate
whose encouragement, support and
love make all things possible –
even this book!

# Contents

*Preface*                                                                                   ix

*Acknowledgements*                                                                          x

1   Marketing and promotions                                                                1
    1.1   Introduction
    1.2   What is marketing?
    1.3   A systematic approach
    1.4   Who are my clients and what do they want?
    1.5   Market segmentation – a key concept
    1.6   The marketing mix
    1.7   Selecting the right image
    1.8   Pricing
    1.9   Applying the theory

2   Understanding money                                                                     27
    2.1   Raising finance
    2.2   How is the business doing now?
    2.3   How to improve performance
    2.4   Increasing sales revenue
    2.5   Controlling direct costs
    2.6   Controlling expenses
    2.7   Acquiring or selling a business

3   Finding staff and keeping them                                                          48
    3.1   Introduction
    3.2   Analysing the job
    3.3   The job description
    3.4   Identifying the right person
    3.5   Analysing the person
    3.6   Attracting potential candidates
    3.7   Initial selection
    3.8   The interview
    3.9   Other methods of selection
    3.10  Terms and conditions of employment
    3.11  Integration of new staff

4   Managing people                                                                         84
    4.1   What is managing?
    4.2   Communication
    4.3   Motivation
    4.4   Behaviour
    4.5   Leadership styles

5   Handling staff problems and disciplinary procedures                                     119
    5.1   Discipline
    5.2   Procedure for producing rules
    5.3   The disciplinary process

   5.4   The disciplinary interview
   5.5   Conclusions

6   Training                                                           129
   6.1   Introduction
   6.2   Identification and analysis of training needs
   6.3   Defining the objectives
   6.4   Planning the programme
   6.5   Evaluating the training

7   Planning and organisation                                          140
   7.1   Planning the salon
   7.2   Planning the work
   7.3   Business planning

8   Managing time and priorities                                       154
   8.1   Planning your time
   8.2   Planning your staff's time

9   The law                                                            161
   9.1   Legislation affecting employment of staff
   9.2   Recruitment
   9.3   Servicing the employment
   9.4   Health and Safety at Work Act 1974

10   The future of the industry                                        164
   10.1   An ageing population
   10.2   Franchising
   10.3   Home hairdressers
   10.4   Shortage of skilled staff
   10.5   Hair product manufacturers

Appendix
   Sources of Information                                              170

Index                                                                 172

# Preface

As we move towards the end of the century our environment and the way in which we work or, indeed, want to work is changing. This raises issues for the future of the hairdressing industry as part of the growth in the service sector.

For many years clients and colleagues have said that there is not enough information available about hairdressing business management written for the people who actually work in hairdressing or who wish to enter hairdressing.

When you first thought about becoming a hairdresser you were probably attracted to the industry because of your creative ability or because you liked the idea of meeting and helping people. One of the other skills that is needed to be a good hairdresser is an eye for detail. If you wish to progress further or learn more about hairdressing business management, this book will show you how important it is to be analytical in your approach to running a salon whether it is to promote the business, recruit the right staff, train and develop them or to make a profit. The skills required are 80 per cent analysis and 20 per cent instinct or intuition.

The ability to analyse can sound very boring but, in fact, just as hairdressers need an eye for detail to create a high quality haircut, that same skill can be adapted successfully to run a salon.

This book has been written from many years' experience of working with and advising salons and companies within hairdressing in all aspects of managing, marketing and training and being able to show them how to successfully apply basic business concepts within the hairdressing industry.

This book also covers the syllabus of the Management Certificate in Hairdressing (part of the Nationally Preferred Scheme in Hairdressing) of which I helped to pilot the scheme, and is essential reading for anyone who wishes to increase their knowledge and confidence by qualifying as a professional manager.

# Acknowledgements

This book has been possible because of the support of many people in the hairdressing industry – people who believed in me and my views on the future of business management in hairdressing, and how tried and tested management training skills could successfully apply to hairdressing businesses.

Along the way, these people were prepared to take the 'risk', as they saw it, of trying new approaches in managing their businesses. It is impossible to name them all but I shall be forever grateful to Felicity Green and Philip Rogers who first introduced me to the world of hairdressing, Remy, Steve Ellis, Derek Green, Patrick Hare, Philip McCarthy, Brian Jarvis and Kevin Arkell who were prepared to try new things.

*Annette Mieske*

# Chapter One
# Marketing and promotions

## 1.1 Introduction

This chapter covers the crucial area of marketing and promotions. It develops the major marketing concepts and applies these to hairdressing businesses. It examines the whole area of promotions and how to make these effective.

Many salon owners spend enormous amounts of time and money in opening a salon but frequently forget that the research required *prior* to selecting a salon is essential if the new venture is to be successful.

Secondly, time and money must be allocated to market and promote the business so that the public, the community, suppliers and potential staff know of its existence.

## 1.2 What is marketing?

In today's climate of increased competition many salon owners realise the need to constantly promote their business. Most would agree that the purpose of promotion is to attract new clients into the salon. But is it? Modern marketing theory would suggest that for a hairdresser, promotion in all its forms including advertising has at least six objectives:

- To inform clients of the services offered
- To attract new clients to the business
- To persuade old clients to come back to the business
- To remind clients that they are doing the right thing by using your business
- To attract new staff and motivate current staff
- To promote your image to competitors, staff, clients etc

Research has shown that all these objectives can be achieved by effective promotional and marketing strategy.

But what is promotion? Is it advertising? Special offers? Shows? Model nights? Yes, all of these and more.

Promotion is one part of a whole approach or philosophy towards the way you run your business. This has sometimes been called the *marketing concept*.

In this book we will adopt a disciplined approach to managing promotion where, as far as possible, myths, hunches or intuition are eliminated or at least tempered with reasoned judgement based on carefully prepared information and statistics – in other words obtaining the facts and analysing them. This is essential if you are to try to make promotions and marketing activity less risky and costly and therefore more likely to succeed.

Our recommended approach hinges on six main steps:

- Analyse

- Define
- Propose
- Evaluate
- Choose
- Execute

Let us now look at these steps in more depth.

## 1.3 A systematic approach

### 1.3.1 Analyse

We must analyse the situation within the business as it is at the present time by collecting as much information as possible in order to give a clear picture.

*Client base*

We show you in Exercise 1.1 how to do a simple analysis in two ways to test what percentage of clients are regular visitors. *The key to any successful business is regular clients*: they are the easiest to sell to and your staff can build up rapport and develop a profitable relationship. Research has shown many reasons why people change salons. There are those who 'always try the new salon' or 'want a change' but often the reasons are simpler:

- The staff aren't rude
- They do a professional job
- The salon is clean
- It has a friendly atmosphere
- They don't keep you waiting
- They don't rip you off with all those *extras* on the bill
- You get treated properly there

We will examine these 'buying reasons', as they are called, in later sections.

---

### Exercise 1.1 Assessing client loyalty

*Method 1*
Examine one month's bookings. Count the following categories:

- Clients for the first time
- Clients who have been 1–5 times before
- Clients who have been 6+ times before (or for over a year)

If you do not know all this just use two simple categories, i.e. new and repeats.

Express these as percentages, i.e.

$$\% \text{ new clients} = \frac{\text{no. of new clients}}{\text{total clients}} \times 100$$

If the salon is not very new or has not recently been expanded, then the higher the percentage of new clients the more concern you need have.

*Method 2*

Only use if you have proper client record cards – (which you should have!). Take every tenth card and calculate how many months the client has been coming to you by completing the table below. If the first card shows 8 months you put a tick in the 7–12 months row, i.e.

|  | Ticks | Nos | % |
|---|---|---|---|
| 1 month or less |  |  |  |
| 1–3 months |  |  |  |
| 4–6 months |  |  |  |
| 7–12 months |  |  |  |
| More than a year |  |  |  |

TOTAL _____

$$\text{Note } \% = \frac{\text{no.}}{\text{total}} \times 100$$

You can check it has been done correctly if the totals of % come to about 100. The more clients you have had for a long time, the healthier your business is (and the more stable).

If you do not have a proper record system then setting this up should be one of the items to put into *action now*!

*Client knowledge*

In order to correctly meet client needs you must have a clear idea of:

- Who your clients are and how many there are
- Why they come to your salon (instead of competitors)
- What the market potential is in your area for your kind of client
- Your own business strengths and weaknesses and your advantages/ disadvantages over your clients

*Meeting business targets*

The third aspect of analysing where you are now is assessing your financial performance. After all, you must want to make money too unless you are running a hairdressing salon because you love clients or as an ego trip! There are three quick measures to see if you are on target:

- Return on capital employed – around 20 per cent
- Gross profit – about 40–50 per cent
- Net profit – about 12–20 per cent

**Exercise 1.2  Stylist's client analysis form**

Branch ...........................................................     Week ending ...........................

Stylist's name

| Day | Rev £ | p | Client | Rev £ | p | Client | Rev £ | p | Client | Rev £ | p | Client | Rev £ | p | Client | Total New | Clients Reg | Total |
|-----|-------|---|--------|-------|---|--------|-------|---|--------|-------|---|--------|-------|---|--------|-----------|-------------|-------|
| Mon | | | | | | | | | | | | | | | | | | |
| Tues | | | | | | | | | | | | | | | | | | |
| Wed | | | | | | | | | | | | | | | | | | |
| Thur | | | | | | | | | | | | | | | | | | |
| Fri | | | | | | | | | | | | | | | | | | |
| Sat | | | | | | | | | | | | | | | | | | |
| Total | | | | | | | | | | | | | | | | | | |
| Average | | | | | | | | | | | | | | | | | | |
| New | | | | | | | | | | | | | | | | | | |
| Reg | | | | | | | | | | | | | | | | | | |

Absentees:                Holidays:                Customer complaints: .........................

Mon
Tues
Wed
Thurs
Fri
Sat

........................................

Manager's notes: ..............................

........................................

Manager's signature: ..............

If you cannot answer the above questions then contact your accountant *now* and ask him the following or read Chapter 2 on Understanding money:

(1) What are my figures for the salon this year?
(2) Have they improved/worsened/stayed the same?
(3) How do they compare with the competition?
(4) Why did he not tell you all this without asking?

*Client services*

You need to know not only how many new and regular clients your salon takes per week or month but which of your staff have the most regular clients and which are booked with the new clients. You need to know that 50 per cent of all *new* clients are being converted over 8–10 weeks to regular clients by individual stylists (see Exercise 1.2 Stylist's client analysis form).

You also need to know which of your services are most used by clients, e.g. cuts, perms, colours, so that you have evidence of what most of the salon and individual's time is devoted to. This subject will be covered in more depth in section 1.8 Pricing.

*Client satisfaction*

You must aim to provide what the client wants. The client is 'boss', not the owner or manager. Too many hairdressers treat clients as something to be tolerated or endured. But how can you tell if you are satisfying your clients?

● Ask them about service
● Analyse client base

*Ask clients about the service*

If you wish to find out what your clients want then you must ask them in such a way that does not embarrass them and by using questioning techniques which will require their honest opinion as opposed to a straightforward yes/no answer.

Exercise 1.3 gives an example of a client satisfaction survey.

Do bear in mind that some clients may be more generous than others in their praise of the salon – so it's never wise to be complacent!

To summarise, marketing is concerned with providing client satisfaction at a profit and requires a knowledge of what clients want and a determination to provide it in a better way than competitors.

These ideas are developed further in later sections where marketing theory is examined and applied to the hairdressing industry.

---

**Exercise 1.3 Client satisfaction survey**
We are constantly trying to improve our service and would be grateful if you could help by telling us where we are good and where we can improve. All your answers will be treated in confidence but will be considered. Thank you for taking the time to complete this survey.

Management

Please ring the number which indicates how you felt about each aspect below. Ring 1 if you felt it was very poor, 2 = poor, 3 = acceptable, 4 = good, 5 = very good/excellent. Please add comments or write overleaf if you wish to say more. Leave an item blank if you do not wish to or cannot answer.

| Item | | Score | | | |
|---|---|---|---|---|---|
| (1) Decoration and appearance of salon | 1 | 2 | 3 | 4 | 5 |
| (2) Comfort (i.e. the temperature of the salon) and cleanliness | 1 | 2 | 3 | 4 | 5 |
| (3) Music and lighting (music too loud etc.) | 1 | 2 | 3 | 4 | 5 |
| (4) Refreshments and reading | 1 | 2 | 3 | 4 | 5 |
| (5) Efficiency of service | 1 | 2 | 3 | 4 | 5 |
| (6) Friendliness of staff | 1 | 2 | 3 | 4 | 5 |
| (7) Quality of service (hairdressing) | 1 | 2 | 3 | 4 | 5 |
| (8) Were the staff informative about our services and products? | 1 | 2 | 3 | 4 | 5 |

Will you come again        YES ☐    NO ☐    If NO, Why not?

What things do you like about this salon? ................................................................

................................................................

What do you think could be improved? ................................................................

What did you have done today? ................................................................

Which member(s) of staff served you? ................................................................

Thank you for completing this survey

---

## 1.4 Who are my clients and what do they want?

Many staff do not stop and think 'what type of clients do I have and where do they come from?' Ask a stylist the reasons why a client visits and they will tend to be very different from the client's reasons. If you are to establish your salon's strengths and weaknesses you need as many facts as possible. Marketing men seem almost obsessed with the answers to the question 'what business are we in?' You would probably answer 'hairdressing'. But are you? If you think hard you will see that the President of Revlon who said 'in the factory we make cosmetics, in the drug store we sell hope' has relevance to the hairdressing industry. Our research has shown that the real reasons that people go to hairdressers are varied and there are no general reasons. If you look at Fig. 1.1 showing some reasons why women go to hairdressers then clearly the choice of salon is directly connected with the reasons and your ability to meet the client's requirements.

**Fig. 1.1** Some reasons why women go to hairdressers (*Street Research* 1982).

 (1) To make them feel good.
 (2) To make them look beautiful and/or younger.
 (3) To get some peace and quiet from the kids.
 (4) To look fashionable.
 (5) To be able to talk to a sympathetic ear.
 (6) To have a nice young man/woman looking after them.
 (7) To get out of the house.
 (8) To spoil themselves – a special treat.
 (9) To make their hair easy-to-manage.
(10) To get a good rest.

If you are to analyse the business you are in, you need to define the three kinds of service that a hairdressing salon offers. These are:

(1) *Tangible service* – the obvious thing you offer – cutting/styling/perming, etc.
(2) *Extended service* – the whole range of interlinked services you offer, e.g. products, fashion advice, hair care and beauty aids, etc.
(3) *Generic service* – the real (often unstated) benefit that the client actually wants from coming to the salon.

The first two kinds of service seem reasonably straightforward but it is the third area, the generic service, which is most volatile and *rapidly changes as a client's needs change*. Marketing research has identified that during the next decade customers' needs will change and it is up to a salon to decide how some of these needs can be met through the services that are offered.

For example more people are now increasingly concerned about their health, i.e. health food, preservatives in food, anti-smoking, what is contained in hair and beauty products. Thus any promotion stressing the positive factors will appeal to people who have these kinds of needs. Young people in particular are very concerned about the environment and health. You may like to think through the implications of some of the other consumer needs and wants for the 1990s for yourself (see Fig. 1.2).

**Fig. 1.2** New aspects of consumer needs and wants in the 1990s.

 (1) More casual lifestyles.
 (2) Desire for elegance and individualism.
 (3) Flexibility of roles, e.g. women's liberation.
 (4) More 'instant gratification' as lifestyle.
 (5) Readier acceptance of credit etc.
 (6) New work ethic ('work to live' not 'live to work').
 (7) Consumerism (quality and value for money is a *right*).
 (8) Shrinking world (acceptance of ethnic groups etc.).
 (9) Rejection of big business ('small *is* beautiful').
(10) Pleasure is good and not immoral.
(11) More leisure time.
(12) Energy conservation/ecology/environmental issues.
(13) Changing morality about all things.
(14) Concern about appearance and health.
(15) Novelty, change and escapism fashionable.
(16) Desire for natural things now important.

## 1.5 Market segmentation – a key concept

Many hairdressers try to be 'all things to all people' and have a wide range of clients. You can compare this with the small corner shop which sold everything. But few people ever 'got rich quick' in a corner shop (and had time to enjoy the fruits of their labours) and those that did copied the ideas of supermarkets by attracting a particular group of clients and tailoring their image to meet those clients' needs. Market segmentation or *client group identification* is a key concept for promotional success.

The market for each type of product or service is unique, e.g. cars, perms or clothing. This individuality is caused by variations in many characteristics, e.g. size of market, pricing structure, characteristics of customers, buying habits etc.

It is essential to analyse the market in which the organisation is interested, in order to establish its characteristics, prior to the formulation of any objectives and plans. The issues that need to be covered include:

(1) What do the clients in the market buy, i.e. what type of product/service and how much of it, how often etc.?
(2) Why does the client buy it, i.e. for what purpose is it purchased and for what reason, e.g. reliability, status, cheapness?
(3) Who purchases the product/service and who does the buying, e.g. in a family is it the wife or husband?
(4) What is the person's buying procedure, e.g. walk-ins, appointments, impulse visits, perms or colour correction, occasional appointments?
(5) When is the purchase made, e.g. half-yearly, once a week during a shopping trip, on holiday, at a particular time of year, when hair is unmanageable?
(6) Where is the product purchased, e.g. retail shops, mail order, superstores, supermarkets, at exhibitions etc.?

Answers to the questions listed above will provide an outline of the market concerned and reveal that there is often more than one answer to each question. This is because clients buying a certain category of product will be very different in their characteristics including buying behaviour and the use to which the product is put.

### Market segmentation – a definition

Market segmentation involves recognition that every market is made up of distinguishable groups consisting of buyers with different needs, methods of buying and responses to variations of what the seller offers. No single item, product or service offered to the market will meet the needs of all buyers. The process of identifying these groups is 'market segmentation'.

### The uses of segmentation

(1) Identification of market opportunities available, i.e. what needs and whose needs. There will be several segments in each market.
(2) Evaluation of opportunities offered by each segment on a logical basis against the firm's objectives, resources and capability. An aid in the selection of which group of buyers to serve, which of their needs and with what offering.

(3) As a basis for planning, executing and monitoring the firm's offering to buyers.

(4) To provide competitive advantage if the firm can identify segments not adequately served by competitors, e.g. a small firm may be able to service a large share of a small specialised segment of the market, which would be uneconomic for a large rival. This may avoid direct confrontation witth powerful competitors in the larger segments. The largest segment does not always offer the greatest opportunity.

To summarise, the stages in developing market segmentation are:

- Identify clear leader segments (or groups) whom you wish to aim at
- Examine the characteristics of those groups in detail and in particular their needs and preferences
- Tailor your whole approach to them
- Promote directly to these segments and sell to them and reap the benefits
- Be constantly aware of changing needs of new segments and act accordingly

See Fig. 1.3 Market segmentation and Fig. 1.4 Five possible segments to exploit.

It is not just in the biggest segment that money is to be made. Ford sell more cars per day than BMW per week, but BMW make more profit. Any segment can be profitable if you (a) identify it and (b) sell to it correctly.

It is not just large companies that do it. The difference between those that make it and those that don't is (a) recognising it and (b) doing it.

You can segment a market in a large number of ways. For example, Fig. 1.3 shows the various segmenting categories and Fig. 1.4 lists a number of segments you might consider as possibilities for marketing and promotional approach.

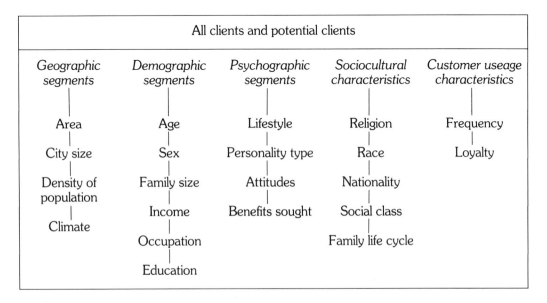

| All clients and potential clients | | | | |
|---|---|---|---|---|
| Geographic segments | Demographic segments | Psychographic segments | Sociocultural characteristics | Customer useage characteristics |
| Area | Age | Lifestyle | Religion | Frequency |
| City size | Sex | Personality type | Race | Loyalty |
| Density of population | Family size | Attitudes | Nationality | |
| Climate | Income | Benefits sought | Social class | |
| | Occupation | | Family life cycle | |
| | Education | | | |

**Fig. 1.3** Market segmentation.

**Fig. 1.4** Five possible segments to exploit.

(1) *Ethnic groups*
'Black' or 'Asian' styles

(2) *Trends*
'Punk' or 'Mod' styles

(3) *Age*
Young teenagers
OAPs
Middle aged
Mothers

(4) *Sex*
Men
Unisex
Women

(5) *Personality type*
Beauty-conscious type. Offer complete service e.g. sunbed, manicure, beauty advice etc.
Price up-market

## 1.6 The marketing mix

In this section we examine one of the most powerful weapons in any business – the marketing mix. This is one of the hardest concepts to understand but it can be applied to almost any situation and can be used to predict the implications of any course of action.

The concept of the marketing mix is simple in that you see the business as a system sitting in an environment competing with other businesses attempting to attract clients from that market – in other words, a salon sitting in a place competing with other hairdressing salons to attract clients.

In order to do this you need to adopt the right marketing mix for the particular segment to which you wish to sell. Marketing experts usually talk about the four 'Ps' of marketing:

- Price
- Place
- Promotion
- Product

The important thing to remember is that you cannot consider any of these four in isolation. Hairdressers who increase or indeed decrease prices without considering the effects on the rest of the mix are likely to be unsuccessful either by losing clients or by attracting too many of the wrong type, e.g. unprofitable ones. But how do you choose the right mix? There are no definite answers. There are a large number of factors, however, which affect the mix.

Figure 1.5 shows in detail the four categories of the marketing mix. What must be done, however, is to analyse clients and their segments together with a detailed profit analysis to identify where turn-over and profit is obtained. In other words, finding out what are your most profitable services and an examination in detail of all of your promotional activities.

**Fig. 1.5**
Marketing mix.

(1) *Product factors (services)*
Product planning (new products/lines) (new styles)
Market segments aimed for – who? what? where? how many?
Innovation (attitudes to)
Expertise of staff

(2) *Price factors*
Competitive prices (in same segments)
Specific price ranges and structures (e.g. higher prices on weekends/holidays?)
Nature and type of discounts (client loyalty discounts)
Pricing policies – how many prices? (Are they too complicated, are they inclusive of conditioners/styling aids?) e.g. school-leaver/OAPs/unemployed
How often are prices reviewed?
Differential pricing on key services (higher prices for blow-dries, lower prices for perms)
Attitudes to credit or accounts etc.

(3) *Promotion*
Sales training for staff
Promotional methods to be used
Amount of money to be spent on all forms of advertising/promotion
Image to be maintained/enhanced
Merchandising/promotion of products where stocked (display material)
Packaging/own branding (where products are sold in quantity)
Competitors' activities

(4) *Place (distribution)*
Location of salon (can it be found?)
Stock control of key items
Parking facilities/transport availability

## 1.7 Selecting the right image

Selecting an image for a salon sounds to many stylists and salon owners like the fun side of starting up a business. In fact, many of them select an image by their own personal taste or style – this can often be a costly mistake.

*What is an image?*

The word 'image' means different things to different people. *The Oxford Dictionary* describes it as a 'likeness, reproduction in the memory of the sensation of sight, hearing and smell'. You should use this interpretation as a useful guideline and consider how you can create an image using sensations of 'sight, hearing and smell' that meet the needs of the majority of your clients with the *segment you wish to attract*.

Let's take each of the senses in turn:

Sight      What can be seen?
Sound      What can be heard, e.g. what kind of atmosphere? How are
           we greeted? What kind of conversation goes on in the salon?
Smell      What smells invade the salon?
Touch      How is our sense of touch affected?
Taste      What do we eat/drink in the salon?

### 1.7.1 Sight

What can we see with our eyes?

*Accessibility*

The position of the salon is the first item to consider.
*Ground floor* – can be seen by potential passing trade. The external
appearance would be essential. Many salons alienate their clients by an 'up-
market' appearance even though their prices are much lower than the
appearance of the salon. Tinted glass, net curtains and blinds all create visual
images that can enhance or detract from the image you wish to create.
*First floor salons* – when walking down your local high street how often do
you look up to another floor or even notice the architecture of the buildings?
Even the most outstanding architecture becomes commonplace when you
shop in the same town regularly. Ensuring a visual impact on the first floor
can be difficult from the outside. This is where concentration on other 'image'
factors should be used.
*Salons in side streets* – immediate accessibility is difficult. Other 'visual' image
methods need to be adopted, e.g. promotions, advertising and public
relations.

*Colour schemes*

When fitting out the salon how did you select the colours? How much
thought did you really give to this? Did you think it should be ultra-modern
or did you look at other salons in the area first to see if your ideas coincided?
The drawback of selecting your favourite colours is that they may be fine for
you, but what about the impact they have on your clients and the *segments*
that you wish to attract?
   Psychologists tell us that certain colours have different effects on mood
and behaviour. Think about the effects of sitting in a grey room. Does it make
you feel depressed? Is it a soft grey which can be relaxing or a hard blue grey
which can be cold and clinical? What effect does red have on you? Does it
cheer you up – or make you feel claustrophobic and aggressive? When
selecting colours decisions need to be made about the atmosphere as well as
the visual impact that colours can have upon your clients and, just as
important, the effect they will have upon your staff who have to work in the
salon every day. So give some thought to colours and the effect they can
have and how they help create a backcloth for the mood and atmosphere of
your business.
   Hairdressers often think that if they are creating fashionable styles salon
fitments should be up-to-the-minute in design, but consider how quickly a
salon dates by having orange or brown backwashes – these can be very

expensive to re-vamp. There are many ways of making salons modern, by changing the colour of the walls, lighting and easily removed fittings, without having to change the essentials such as flooring, styling positions and styling chairs. It is often possible to tell when a salon was opened by the colour schemes and fitments – unless the owner had the foresight to be aware of future colour trends.

When selecting a colour scheme it should be used or co-ordinated within gowns, towels and stationery such as appointment cards and price lists. Otherwise the image created confuses not only the public but potential employees whom you will also need to attract.

*Printing*

Hairdressers fall too easily into the trap of thinking they should be experts in everything. Some salon owners have tremendous talent for design and visual impact, but do not consider the nitty-gritty like the quality of the printing. Printing and typesetting should be left to other professionals but beware of back street printers who imply that the more expensive printers are ripping off their clients. This is not always the case. There are exceptions in every business but it is usual to get what you pay for. Bear in mind that selecting unusual colours for the interior of the salon, equipment and printing could escalate the production cost in all these items.

*Salon names and logos*

Selecting a name needs considerable thought. These are the guidelines to follow:

- Keep it timeless. These examples indicate different decades:

  Maison Fred
  Cut and Blow
  Curl Up and Dye
  Head Shavers

  Old-fashioned names do not encourage new clients

- Tell clients what you offer, e.g. hair cutting, colouring, perming, dressing, service, products, expertise.
- Don't let the name of the salon grow old like the salon owner unless it is synonomous with success, e.g. Vidal Sassoon or Mister Michael, John Thomas etc.
- Select a name consistent with the image you wish to adopt for the client segment you want to attract, e.g.

  Barnetts!
  Coiffure!
  Hair!

- Think about how the name can be written in an attractive form to remind people of who you are.
- Use a 'pay-off line' or slogan in advertising or promotional material, e.g. 'Philip's Hair Studio – We Care More'.
- Use the logo and pay-off line in all your sales/advertising material to get your message across, e.g. 'Beanz Meanz Heinz'.

*Advertising/sales material*

Play on the theme and image you have created whenever and wherever possible:

- Appointment cards
- Letter headings
- Price lists
- Staff tee-shirts
- Company cars
- Products
- Gowns/towels

- Coffee/tea cups
- Magazine folders
- Hair care leaflets
- Advertising space
- Job vacancies
- Model posters

Look at the classified ads at the back of the trade press – which ones would attract you to apply for a job? When advertising use the following guidelines:

- Don't overcrowd – white space says a lot about your image.
- Use only one or two typefaces and not several, which confuse the message.
- Lay it out attractively.
- Remember *who will be reading it* and give them the information that will make them contact you.
- Keep the message simple.
- Don't try to achieve too many things.

*The staff*

There is no point spending time and money on a coherent image if your staff do not reflect it in terms of:

- Appearance – clothes and hair
- Manner/behaviour to each other and to the clients
- Standards of work
- Standards of service

Encompass all of the above – *your staff are your image. Train them to get it right.*

*Products*

Products can enhance or detract from your image so choose carefully, particularly a retail range.

(1) Manufacturers
    Check out the following:

    - Packaging
    - Support material/hair care leaflets/show cards
    - Training support
    - Prices – ask yourself if they reflect your image

(2) Own brand

    - Will the labelling and packaging compliment your image or conflict? Is the product better than a manufacturer's range or the same? (or worse?)

- What price should be charged? The same as a manufacturer, cheaper or more expensive? (Consider the effects of selling very cheap products in an up-market salon.)
- Will staff believe in them? If they don't how will you sell them?
- Consider the capital outlay of packaging and purchasing of stock.

*Photographs*

Do the photographs displayed in the salon emphasise the type of work covered – commercial, avante garde – or are they just pretty pictures to fill up the window? Photographs and display material quickly discolour and should be changed regularly. Unless tatty display material reflects your image!

### 1.7.2 Sound

What can be heard?

*Atmosphere*

It is hard to measure atmosphere but clients and staff know when they feel comfortable with the sounds in the salon.

- *Music.* What type of music? Does it suit the clients or staff? What image does it create?
- *Conversation.* The dialogue between staff and clients – is it happy and bubbly or stressful and aggressive? Are clients included in the conversation? Is the conversation informative or flotsam? 'How were your hols Mrs Smith?' *or* 'How did you get on with your perm Mrs Smith?' Which conversation will be most fruitful to the business? The flotsam may be necessary as a 'warm-up' conversation but how the client copes with her hair and products is more constructive to both parties.
- *Silence.* Silence can be positive or negative. Think about the effect on clients when stylists don't talk to them.
- *Noise.* Noise can be disruptive and for many clients it is uncomfortable when they do not hear what the stylist is saying.
- *Listening.* You may ask how listening can reflect the image of the salon. If we do not listen to what a client says how can we find out her needs? More salons lose clients by not listening to what the client wants than probably any other area of the business. You must learn to listen by asking open questions and checking you have understood and agreed a course of action. Read Section 4.2 Communication.

*Answering the telephone*

You should never underestimate the value of how the telephone is answered – indeed, who does answer it? Is it the youngest, most inexperienced trainee or someone who has been trained properly to answer the telephone? If the salon does not have a receptionist then it is essential that all staff are trained in how to answer the telephone and the range of questioning techniques that can be used to extract information from people as well as make them feel welcome.

*Welcome!*

When clients walk into a salon how are they greeted? Do the staff look at the client as if they are an interruption to the work they are already carrying out? Or are they greeted with a smile and by name? Are they helped with their coat and gown? How many salons offer consultation prior to having their hair shampooed at the backwash? Remember, it is the first impression that counts, particularly with new clients visiting the salon. It is the new clients that see the salon as it really is.

*Client interest*

What kind of conversation goes on in the salon? Is the conversation about holidays and what everyone saw on the TV the night before or, is it about how the client copes with her hair? What products does she use on her hair? How does she dry it? How does she cope with it? How has she handled her hair since the last perm, colour or treatment? The business that you are really in is not hairdressing but the business of offering knowledge and information so that clients can cope with their hair between salon visits. An interesting concept and anathema to many people in the hairdressing industry!

### 1.7.3 Smell

What smells invade the salon? How can smell reflect our image? The smell of products, people and equipment can be attractive to clients. Check the following:

- Adequate heating and ventilation to ensure a comfortable atmosphere
- Cleanly laundered gowns and towels – not dried-off towels smelling of perm solution and the give-away musty smell of re-dried towels!
- Pleasant-smelling products – more people today are concerned with the use of chemicals than at any other time
- Sweet-smelling staff – at the backwash and particularly those staff who have a taste for alcohol, garlic and curries!

### 1.7.4 Touch

How is our sense of touch affected when we are in a hairdressing salon?

- Gowns – do they feel pleasant to touch?
- Surfaces – do they feel clean or sticky?
- Products – are we allowed to touch the products? Are they available to be touched at a styling position?
- Client contact – do we touch our clients in a friendly, reassuring way? When does the touch become a grope or sexual overture? The line is a fine one and we need to train staff in body contact and body signals in order that they understand clients' responses.

### 1.7.5 Taste

What is eaten or drunk in the salon? If you are going to offer drinks to your clients then ensure that the coffee tastes of coffee, that the tea tastes of tea and that it is served in cups that do not taste of washing-up liquid or another client's lipstick.

Consumer trends for the 1990s indicate healthy, natural and preservative-free food and drink wherever possible. Does the salon offer herbal teas, decaffeinated coffee, fresh orange juice and bottled water? If sandwiches are offered, are they on wholemeal bread – in other words, are clients given a wider choice than just standard tea or coffee? More importantly, when the food or drink is served does it taste good?

In conclusion, image is definable and measurable if you consider all the points raised above. By being aware of these things you can ensure you remain in control of what can so easily slip from our grasp.

## 1.8 Pricing

Pricing is probably one of the most important factors of running any hairdressing salon – and the one with which most people in the hairdressing industry have problems. From my own experience in working in consultancy within the industry for a number of years, pricing is the one area that the vast majority of salons get wrong. Yet it is the one, if calculated properly, that is the key to success and profitability and makes marketing and promoting the salon easier.

The factors you need to consider in deciding your prices are many and include:

- Competition
- Market acceptance
- Your own costs
- Your image
- What you wish to achieve by your pricing strategy

Research shows that hairdressers are reluctant to price up, in case they lose clients. Yet, given a higher profit on each price, it is possible to lose clients and still emerge eventually better off in profit terms. But how do you balance all of these factors? You need to examine each of them in turn.

### 1.8.1 Competition

Clearly you wish to be competitive but you must ensure that you are comparing 'like with like'. If you are up-market, giving a good service and extras to clients, then you may be able to command a higher price in the market place, e.g. compare Tesco and Marks and Spencer! You can check competition both in terms of price and service either by visiting or 'sending in' someone to find out for you. This 'military intelligence' approach is common in other types of business and can provide useful information. You can look at other aspects while you are there. Some hairdressers use wives, girlfriends, friends or relatives to do this. What is essential is that a hairdresser, particularly the salon owner, does not analyse or visit competitors' salons. The reason for this is that hairdressers are always biased against other hairdressers and their services. They very rarely judge the services objectively and are often very critical of each other's services and hairdressing. Clients who are not hairdressers judge services by the way they

**Fig. 1.6**
Checking out your
competitors.

| Item | Us | Competitor 1 | Competitor 2 | Competitor 3 |
|---|---|---|---|---|
| (1) Prices (Include what) | | | | |
| (2) Quality of work | | | | |
| (3) Type of client (Young mums, professional people and age range) | | | | |
| (4) Image projected | | | | |
| (5) Extras provided (Inclusive of coffee, fruit juice, conditioner, style aids) | | | | |
| (6) Other factors (Cleanliness, atmosphere, appearance of staff) | | | | |

are treated upon a visit and the standard of the hairdressing is judged by the following:

(1) Whether it was what the client wanted.
(2) Whether he/she can manage it at home.
(3) The knowledge and advice they were given to help keep their hair in the same style and condition in between salon visits.

To analyse competitors in a simple way see Fig. 1.6.

### 1.8.2 Market acceptance

This is clearly a key factor. In a poor area you cannot command the high prices that central town salons do and in areas of high unemployment high prices would make for difficulties. However, many segments will still pay more than others and various kinds of differential pricing are worth considering, e.g.:

(1) Charging more at holiday times, weekends and other busy times
(2) Charging less on quiet days
(3) Special categories, e.g. school leavers, OAPs, unemployed etc.
(4) Offering a special 'Rolls Royce' service

Basically, from this approach it is 'what the market will bear' that is really important.

### 1.8.3 Your own costs

The problem here is two-fold:

(1) Determining your costs properly

(2)  Interpreting the cost data in a meaningful way so as to lead to realistic pricing

Costing is described more fully in Chapter 2 Understanding money but suffice it to say here that there are a number of different kinds of cost which are confusingly similar in definition. Two useful ones are *unit cost* and *full cost*. For this you need to understand and calculate the following information explained more fully in Chapter 2:

- Gross profit which should ideally be 45–48 per cent
- Net profit – in the hairdressing industry, usually 10–15%
- Return on capital employed

In calculating pricing you must understand the idea of contribution, e.g.

Contribution = selling price – variable costs

**Fig. 1.7** Income statement.

| Income statement | Company XYZ | Period 1989 | | | |
|---|---|---|---|---|---|
| (1) Sales (turnover) excl. VAT | | | | | 50,000 |
| (2) Cost of sales | | | | | |
|     Materials | 2,500 | | | | |
|     Wages/salaries | 25,000 | | | | 27,500 |
| | | | Gross profit | | 22,500 |
| | | | | | (45%) |
| (3) Expenses | | | | | |
|     Salon operating | | | | | |
|       Rent, rates and water | | 5,000 | | | |
|       Repairs and renewals | | 1,000 | | | |
|       Light and heat | | 400 | | | |
|       Insurances | | 100 | 6,500 | | |
|     Salon administration | | | | | |
|       Telephone | | 300 | | | |
|       Accountancy and audit | | 300 | | | |
|       Stationery and postage | | 200 | | | |
|       Advertising/promotion | | 2,000 | 2,800 | | |
|     Motor vehicle costs | | | | | |
|       Running expenses | | 1,200 | | | |
|       Leasing/hire | | 2,800 | 4,000 | | |
|     Financial charges | | | | | |
|       Bank interest and charges | | 700 | 700 | | |
|     Depreciation | | 1,000 | 1,000 | 15,000 | |
| n.b. Capital = 5,000 | | | Net profit | 7,500 | |
| | | | | (15%) | |

These figures are exemplary only.

In the hairdressing business, variable costs are made up of two main elements:

(1) Wages/salaries including employer's National Insurance contributions
(2) Consumables – stock, coffee/tea included in the price, supply of laundry per client etc.

If you look at Fig. 1.7 you will see that this business has a 45 per cent gross profit, a 15 per cent net profit and that wages and materials amount to 55 per cent of turnover. Wages, including employer's National Insurance contributions, should never be higher than 53 per cent and within the range of 40–53 per cent. If the figure is much lower then this means one of three things:

(1) Staff are underpaid
(2) Staff are being paid 'under the table' or cash-in-hand
(3) The owner or manager of the business is working harder than anyone else generating turnover (takings) in order to pay the wages of the staff!

*Break-even*

We must now introduce another new concept, that of break-even volume where we define

$$\text{Break-even} = \frac{\text{Total fixed costs}}{\text{Contribution}} \text{ (or Expenses)}$$

which in this case this amounts to

$$\frac{£15\,000}{0.45} = £33\,333$$

Break-even means the turnover that you must make to cover your costs which in our example gives us £33 333. We call the difference between actual turnover and break-even turnover the 'margin of safety', i.e.

$$£50000 - £33\,333 - £16\,667$$

This is the amount by which sales can fall before actually losing money. The higher the margin, the less vulnerable one is to competition. If prices are increased then the break-even goes down and it is possible to estimate what sales are needed to equate new and old profit levels. This is the basis of 'contribution or break-even' pricing.

*Example*
Suppose XYZ Company increased its prices by 10 per cent (exclusive of VAT) without changing its costs.

|  | Before price increase | 10% price increase |
|---|---|---|
| Sales | 50,000 | ? |
| Contribution (per £) | 0.45 | 0.55 |
| Fixed costs | 15,000 | 15,000 |
| Net profit | 7,500 | ? |
| Break-even | 33,000 | 27,300 |

Thus break-even sales have fallen because more contribution has been made per sale. To generate £7500 profit with new prices we need to sell about £41 000 of services. Therefore, even if turnover drops by 20 per cent or so we would still make the same profit! (For less work.) Thus raising prices by 10 per cent allows (in our example) a drop of 20 per cent in turnover before profits change. If we translate this into clients by assuming an average of £5 each before increase and £5.50 after:

> before we needed 10 000 clients to make £7500 profit
> after we need only 7,500 clients to make £7500 profit
> i.e. 25 per cent less.

### 1.8.4 *Your image*

You must price according to the image you are putting forward, e.g. if you are up-market then you need to price accordingly. In fact, some research in the USA has indicated that many clients perceive a higher price to indicate a higher standard for the same product within a 10–15 per cent range. Thus by pricing a service too low people may actually believe it to be inferior to a higher priced equivalent service. This, we feel, is a hairdresser's major mistake and reduces profits. Consumers' perceptions of price come from various sources but a number of factors do affect 'what consumers will pay' and their concept of 'value for money':

(1) The image of the salon including:

- Appearance/decor/ambience
- Comfort and furnishings
- Quality of product – cuts, perms etc.
- Staff dress standards etc.

(2) Staff attitudes/professionalism and friendliness, i.e. quality of total services offered. Time spent on *them* is also an important factor – time spent by the stylist and not the most junior member of staff who is allocated to shampoo, neutralise perms and apply tints! Many clients are unhappy with being passed around on a production line basis from one so-called 'specialist' to another.

(3) Amount of advertising/promotion. Promotion offsets the negative effects of price and reinforces the image. If the salon only advertises its business when it is offering discounts on prices or colours then this is the only image that the public will have of that particular salon. Promotions reinforcing the image are much more powerful than offering discounts.

(4) Things included in price:

- Drinks
- Conditioners/styling aids
- Leaflets on haircare advice
- Free samples of retail products

(5) If your salon is up-market then you should avoid having 'scruffy' clientele or staff around the place. It is no coincidence that 'up-market' stores, e.g. Harrods etc. have high standards for all aspects of their business.

**Fig. 1.8** Uses of pricing.

(1) Launching or promoting a new style or product (*initial pricing*) or to a new segment e.g. OAPs.
(2) 'Killing off' a style or product (*'sell off'*).
(3) Promoting your image, i.e. setting the right price for your particular market and the particular image you wish to put across.
(4) 'Skimming or creaming' policy. This is where one uses a high price initially (to maximise profit) and then reduces price when competitors come in or sales fall off.
(5) 'Penetration pricing'. A low price initially to attract high volume or to *compete strongly*, i.e. eliminate competitors. Then when well established allow price to drift up and profit percentages to improve.
(6) 'Charm pricing'. An approach where prices have a certain 'charm' e.g. £4.99 not £5.00, £3.75 not £4 etc. These are more 'attractive' than natural prices.
(7) 'Responsive pricing'. Responding to competition and competitors' prices (see Fig 1.9).
(8) 'Irritation pricing'. Moving prices about may cause competition great problems and particularly if discounts or vouchers are readily given, it may cause confusion among competition. It needs to be watched carefully because it must not irritate clients as well.

### 1.8.5 *What you wish to achieve by your pricing strategy*

The owner or manager of the business must think through the consequences of a pricing strategy and we list below the different types of pricing strategy and the effect that these can have upon a salon. We have listed details in Fig. 1.8 but we examine two examples below:

(1) Differential pricing – certain days are always more busy than others. One can use differential pricing to:

  • Attract clients to quiet days, e.g. discount
  • Detract clients from busy days by premium prices, e.g. increases; or
  • Both

  Differential pricing is a powerful technique generally ignored by hairdressers and one which clearly is advantageous in maximising profit and adjusting demand to supply.
(2) 'Skimming' or 'creaming' – a possible approach here is to identify a new segment and to prepare a product-package at a premium price with promotion until competition responds with a lower price, then subsequently reduce the price to lower levels (after you have recouped your investment), e.g. a new, exciting style.

The effect of price changes on competitors is interesting. Research has shown that clients may perceive price decreases in terms of:

(1) Product or service is outmoded
(2) Product or service is defective and is not selling well
(3) The business has financial problems
(4) Price will come down further if we wait
(5) Quality has been reduced

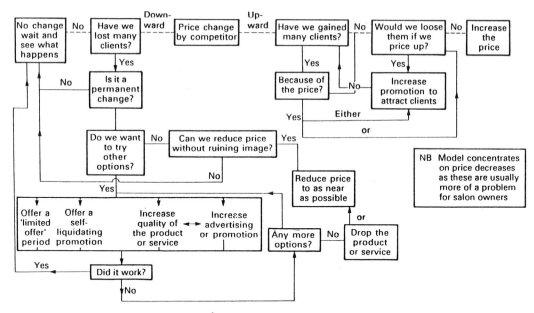

**Fig. 1.9** Price change model – competitive response.

They may perceive price increases as:

(1) Product or service was exceptionally good value and is now reasonable
(2) Product or service is 'burning' and may only be available for a short time
(3) Product or service has been improved
(4) Inflation increases only

Competitors' response is variable too. Many competitors will move only in case of a reduction. Others automatically follow. Clearly where there is less competition there may be little problem. In some areas hairdressers have agreed collectively to raise prices where profits are low or the market is poor.

So how do you respond when a competitor increases his prices? It is a complex process but we offer a model, shown in Fig. 1.9, containing possible guidelines. Ask the questions:

(1) Why has he increased prices?
(2) Is it temporary or permanent?
(3) What are other competitors doing?
(4) Have many clients switched to us as a result? Evidence shows that 'regulars' do tend to be loyal!
(5) Has the service/image changed?
(6) What are my preferences in response?

It is important to try to understand his motives before responding. Is he losing money?

Finally, when considering what the owner or manager is trying to achieve with his/her pricing strategy, we must also consider how long the salon owner, in particular, wishes to remain in business. Does the salon owner intend to get rich quick – which is perfectly possible within a three-year time span – and sell the business and move into other industries outside hairdressing? Alternatively, does the salon owner wish to have a business that will grow over a long period of time with an increased reputation for being fair and professional but also one that will attract staff and clients who wish to be associated with the salon? What is essential is to understand that it is not possible to 'have one's cake and eat it'!

## 1.9 Applying the theory

So far in this chapter we have mentioned a number of areas where we recommend the collection of information. There are four key areas of information which will help in marketing and promoting the business. These are:

(1) Information on clients
(2) Information on competitors
(3) Information on products
(4) Information on staff

### 1.9.1 Information on clients

- Name
- Address
- Telephone number
- Birthday (not year)
- Estimated age group/market segment
- Preferred products/services (from client record card and information from stylist)
- Frequency of visits
- Children's ages
- Usual colour/hair type

This allows you to know your clients, provides you with a mailing list for promotional purposes and allows you to monitor your ability to retain clients.

### 1.9.2 Information on competitors

- Location/image/type of salon
- Number of staff employed
- Prices for services/products
- Assessment of strengths and weaknesses versus your own salon
- Estimate of turnover, e.g. how busy/number of chairs/number of staff

### 1.9.3 Information on products

- Manufacturers' literature on products
- Summary of features and benefits of products
- Detailed instruction on use or limitations
- Price information/costs (not for publication to clients)

This information should be available for every product and service in the salon.

### 1.9.4 Information on staff

- Training required/received
- Selling/commission record
- Has selling and selling training occurred?
- Have they been coached or counselled on any problems which have occurred?
- How do they compare with other staff?

This kind of information provides the basis for business planning, see Section 7.3 Business planning, and for good decision making in the area of promoting the business.

### 1.9.5 Promotional ideas

(1) Try one new promotion every month. Monitor the success and repeat successful ones.
(2) Experiment with salon hours. Close during low periods. Train staff/ clean up the salon. Try evening appointments using special pricing if staff are willing.
(3) Advertise within the salon. Use posters and photographs to show what you have to offer. Keep them in line with your image.
(4) Encourage your staff to sell up, i.e. perms and tints and retail products. Pay them a bonus whenever they do.
(5) Research your customers. Analyse results, seek criticism/complaints. Act on it. Retrain staff. Help them, don't criticise them.
(6) Ring up your own salon and make an appointment (or get a friend to do it). Would you go there? No? Improve it now. Train your staff in handling calls from clients.
(7) Send clients (including ex-clients) a birthday or Christmas card.
(8) Introduce credit cards or cashcards or even accounts for key customers. It's a bit tiresome but research shows clients spend more!
(9) Give all new clients a leaflet or letter thanking them for coming and a small gift (or discount voucher for the next time) for coming. They will love it and come back.
(10) Give all existing clients a 'bring a friend' (and they get the service half price) offer (on less busy days). See how many new clients you can get and keep.
(11) Introduce differential pricing. Charge more on busier days, less on quieter days. Offer discounts on quieter days, i.e. charge more for shampoo/sets and shampoo/blow dries on Fridays and Saturdays, less at the beginning of the week.
(12) Introduce self-service retail sales racks with products near the stylists' working area. Train staff to mention retail sales to all clients.
(13) Train staff in client-handling and selling skills. Many manufacturers offer training free-of-charge and the standards can be good.
(14) Keep in close contact with suppliers. Write and thank them when they are good. Write and complain when they are not. You will be amazed by the results! (Even from the biggest companies.)
(15) Use your window space effectively. It should be clean, tidy, professional. Look at yours. Would it attract you into the salon or send you running off home? Remember it's your public image. No grotty handwritten posters advertising models or reduced prices.

(16) Eliminate unused space. Look at the use of posters, photographs, information to enhance areas. Ensure it's in keeping with your image however.

(17) Say 'thank you' to regular clients. A gift, birthday or Christmas card or even a special letter/note/leaflet just to remind them that you care. 'They take me for granted' is the commonest reason for client dropout!

(18) Introduce a staff suggestion scheme. Give a cash prize for the best successful new idea. Staff can often solve your problems, as they see the alternative ways to tackle them.

(19) Try ringing up some ex-clients inviting them to some special offer or promotion. People love a personal approach.

(20) If you are in a city-centre location, do you have a parking area? Or an inexpensive car park nearby? Then offer a 'get your hair done, free parking all day' deal. Many families might come shopping.

(21) Give a free hair colour/condition and advice offer or invite clients in for coffee (on quiet days). You will be amazed at how many will buy.

(22) Try promoting one of your staff each month in your window. Name/age/biography/interests/work samples. People are fascinated.

(23) Give your staff *name* badges. Clients like to deal with *people*.

(24) Put leaflets in schools, hospitals, colleges, hotels offering special offers on special days.

(25) Display some *before* photographs versus *after* material to show your expertise.

(26) Try a client relations group, i.e. a few regular prominent clients who meet to discuss possible improvements to the salon.

(27) Special offers for particular groups, e.g. 60s women, new job/interview, newly married, brides to be, twenty-first birthdays. Don't worry if people cheat.

(28) Give regular clients (and new ones) a booklet and each time they come stick on a stamp which they can cash in at any time, e.g. 1 stamp = 10% off, 2 stamps = 20% off. It builds loyalty.

(29) If you sell lots of retail products or have a big salon examine your 'own brand'. It might pay off, but the packaging should reflect your image, and the staff must believe in the products.

(30) Introduce the notion of 'standby' or 'apex' haircuts, i.e. low price if you turn up and/or wait for a cancellation. Issue 'ticket' and provide a free 'drink', e.g. wine.

(31) Promote special groups, e.g. twins or working wives, and offer gift/discounts/vouchers, especially if it links in with local events, e.g. all clients who wear a football scarf etc.

(32) Run *joint promotions* with local supermarkets or OAP centre for mums or OAPs.

(33) Run *joint promotions* with discos or record shops or fashion shops especially if you wish to attract trendier youngsters.

(34) Do something 'freaky' occasionally, e.g. have an 'owner and pet' evening or a 'singles' evening and attract an unusual segment.

# Chapter Two
# Understanding money

## 2.1 Raising finance

It does not matter how good the idea, service or hairdressing is likely to be in a new salon or how hard working and skilful the staff – the business will not succeed unless it has sufficient funds. But what constitutes sufficient funds? This depends to a large extent upon what the salon owner wishes to achieve. It depends upon how quickly the salon owner wishes to grow, and on the type of image he or she wishes to project, which will have a direct effect upon the range of equipment and fitments that need to be purchased. It also depends upon another factor which is much more subjective – that is the amount of personal income the salon owner is willing to forgo in order to reap long term financial rewards.

When considering raising finance we have to look at the amount of control over the business the owner is prepared to give up as well as the rate of interest the business will be paying to raise the finance. This factor is much more subjective and emotional in a smaller business than in a larger, well established business. The key sources of funds are:

(1) shares or share capital (limited companies)
(2) loans or loan capital
(3) current liabilities (short term debts)

and we shall see that there are advantages and disadvantages to each.

### The risk element

When you are trying to raise finance a potential source of finance will consider not only the proposal itself but also the past record of the salon or the individuals concerned. Different sources of finance will weigh past performance against future prospects in different ways. In a new salon or new venture the risk is automatically assumed to be greater and therefore the cost of borrowing will be higher. Banks and other financial institutions will want to do business with you if they possibly can – after all that is how banks make their money, upon the interest rates they charge. But they have to feel assured that the risk will be secured in some way. Often a condition of financial support from an outside source may be that adequate life assurance should be taken out or that one's home must be set against the loan as security.

We have listed at the back of this book information regarding potential sources of finance.

### Principal sources of finance

In general, the most important source of finance for a small business is the salon owner's! If the owner's capital is insufficient to provide an adequate base it will not normally be possible for the salon to raise outside finance. In other words, we cannot borrow all the money from a financial institution without being prepared to invest our own cash or personal security against a loan. This reassures the lender that the salon owner is serious about the venture and is prepared to risk his or her own finances.

## Property

Your most important asset may well be your own home. Most people have a mortgage on their property but as the property value rises, it is possible to borrow against any increase in value. Building societies are the cheapest source of mortgage funds, but invariably see their role as providing first mortgages to owner-occupiers. Second mortgages are available from a number of organisations which advertise nationally. If your first mortgage is small, you may be able to raise 70 per cent or more of the value of your house with no restrictions. Professional mortgage brokers do exist but look very carefully, not only at the true rate of interest, but also at the conditions attached to the loan.

## Relatives and friends

These are a potential source of finance for one's new business, but money from this quarter can be a mixed blessing. First, can you be sure that the people concerned are really able to afford the loss of their money if things go wrong? Secondly, would the person involved adopt a professional attitude towards his/her investment by striking a balance between interfering in your business and complete indifference to the utilisation of their money? Thirdly, is it likely that the investor would wish to withdraw his or her money from your firm at short notice? If so, could you allow for this and what would be the effect on your business?

A way of minimising these difficulties would be to ask the friend or relative to act as a guarantor of a bank loan rather than put money into the business directly. However, a tangible support of the guarantee would probably be required.

## Bank loans

Many well known clearing banks such as the Big Four are major sources of finance for small businesses and will, under certain conditions, help finance a new business. They will insist upon safeguarding the security of their loan by either property or the fixed assets within the firm.

## Hire purchase and leasing

It is possible to buy many types of equipment on hire purchase. The procedure is much the same as with domestic hire purchase and the principle is identical. The purchaser pays the deposit or initial payment to the finance company or supplier of goods. The purchaser then takes possession of the goods or equipment once they have signed the hire purchase agreement.

Leasing is similar in that a regular flow of small, equal payments over a fixed period replaces a lump sum purchase, but the goods remain the property of the leasing company at the end of the period. There is no formal agreement that the lease will be renewed or the goods sold to the customer, but either procedure may be followed in return for a nominal sum.

Wella is a manufacturer who can supply fixtures and fittings through its subsidiary 'Welonda Serventi' and may also be able to help with advantageous financial arrangements.

## 2.2 How is the business doing now?

*Understanding the basic documents*

To you, your business probably consists of staff and clients, one providing a service to the other in exchange for money which goes to pay bills and hopefully will make you rich and help your business to expand and grow. To a financial expert, your business is a large box which takes in cash and gives out cash.

In financial terms we do not talk about *cash* but about sales or turnover and costs and/or overheads.

*Profit*

To you, the meaning of profit will be clear – it is what is left at the end of paying all the bills as follows:

Sales/Turnover minus All costs equals Profit

but you need to understand not so much how the money comes in, because in a hairdressing business it comes in through the services you offer, but where the money goes. In order to monitor and control the business you need to keep records which will help you to understand how the money comes in and how it is spent. You need to examine the two main published documents of most businesses – the *balance sheet* and the *profit and loss account* (trading and profit and loss account). These tend to be limited in what they tell you but they do give you some insight into your business.

*The balance sheet*

The balance sheet is best described as a 'snapshot in time' of:

● Where the money in the business has come from (liabilities or sources)
● Where it is currently being used (assets or uses)

The business, in other words, gets its money from the sources and places it in the uses.

**Fig. 2.1** Balance
sheet of Headlines
Ltd.

Balance sheet at 31 January 1990[1]

| Capital | £ | Fixed assets | £ | £ |
|---|---|---|---|---|
| Share capital[2] | 2,500 | Fixtures and fittings | 2,000 | |
| | | Motor vehicle | 1,000 | |
| | | | | 3,000 |
| Loans | | Current assets | | |
| Bank loan | 2,000 | Stock | 700 | |
| | | Debtors | 500 | |
| Current liabilities | | Cash | 800 | |
| Creditors | 500 | | | |
| | | | | 2,000 |
| | 5,000[3] | | | 5,000 |

[1] Balance sheet is always at a point in time.
[2] Probably put in by *you*.
[3] Notice the balance: Assets = Liabilities, i.e. Uses = Sources.

*Sources of funds*
The key sources of funds are:

● Shares or share capital
● Loans or loan capital
● Current liabilities, e.g. creditors

*Uses of funds* are:
Fixed assets – things which are bought to make the business possible such
   as work tops, backwashes, chairs, driers and property if bought freehold,
   e.g. fixtures and fittings, premises, motor vehicles.
Current assets – things which are used in the business, e.g. cash, stock,
   debts.

The balance sheet for a hairdressing business might look like Fig. 2.1.

*The profit and loss account*

The second document, the profit and loss account (or income statement)
gives the recent history of the business and describes how well you have
actually done. It also gives you clues as to where you may go in the future.
Figure 2.2 shows a sample of a profit and loss account (or income statement).

*Cash flow forecast*

The third document can be considered as the crystal ball which reflects the
*exact timing of payments* and sales/turnover coming into the business and
allows you to plan your cash requirements. It must also tally with the bank
deposits or overdraft. The objective of completing this form is that you enter
income or sales and payments only when you actually receive or pay them.
For example, if you receive an electricity bill for the period January to March
on 5 April which you pay in May it would not be shown in your cash flow

**Fig. 2.2** Profit
and loss account.

Headlines Ltd
Profit and loss account (income statement)        Period: 1 year

| | | £ | | |
|---|---|---|---|---|
| (1) Sales   (Turnover) ex VAT | | | | 80,000 |

(2) Cost of sales                          £
      Consumables[1]          4,000
      Wages/salaries         40,000
      (incl. employer's N.I. contributions)     Gross profit    $\underline{44,000}$
                                                              $\overline{36,000}$ (45%)

(3) Expenses
      Salon operating                    £          £
        Rent, rates and water        8,000
        Repairs and renewals           800
        Light and heat                 800
        Insurances                     $\underline{400}$      10,000

      Salon administration
        Telephone                    1,200
        Accountancy and audit fees   1,200
        Stationery and postage       1,200
        Advertising/promotion        $\underline{4,400}$      8,000

      Motor vehicle costs
        Running expenses             1,000
        Leasing/hire                    –        1,000

      Financial charges
        Bank interest and charges     $\underline{600}$        600

      Depreciation                   $\underline{2,000}$     $\underline{2,000}$     $\underline{21,600}$

                                  Net profit             14,400 (18%)

[1] Consumables are materials used in the salon for hairdressing.

statement until May – in other words when you actually pay it.

The cash flow forecast is particularly useful for showing when you need to have cash available or need to borrow cash and banks expect you to have this kind of document available when they lend money (as it also shows when you plan to pay them back). Figure 2.3 is an example of a cash flow forecast.

These three documents together:

● Balance sheet
● Profit and loss account
● Cash flow forecast

give an overall picture of the money in the business, where it came from, what it was used for or invested in, how the business has been performing over the past trading period and how it is managing its cash now and in the future.

It is these three documents that will tell you how well you are doing now and will give you a clear indication of what the strengths and weaknesses are within your business. They do, however, have limitations and you need to examine other ways of collecting information to tell you how well or badly the business is doing.

**Fig. 2.3** Cash flow forecast.

| Item | Jan | Feb | Mar | Apr | May | June |
|---|---|---|---|---|---|---|
| Income | | | | | | |
|   Cash sales | | | | | | |
|   Credit sales | | | | | | |
|   Other income | | | | | | |
| Total income | | | | | | |
| | | | | | | |
| Expenditure | | | | | | |
|   Wages/salaries | | | | | | |
|   Commission | | | | | | |
|   National insurance | | | | | | |
| VAT | | | | | | |
| Taxation | | | | | | |
| Fees | | | | | | |
|   Goods (consumables) | | | | | | |
|   Stock for resale | | | | | | |
|   Rent/lease | | | | | | |
| Rates | | | | | | |
| Gas | | | | | | |
| Electricity | | | | | | |
| Water | | | | | | |
| Telephone | | | | | | |
|   Laundry | | | | | | |
| Stationery | | | | | | |
| Postage | | | | | | |
|   Advertising/promotions | | | | | | |
|   Staff training | | | | | | |
| Staff travel | | | | | | |
|   Motor expenses | | | | | | |
| Servicing/repairs | | | | | | |
| Leasing | | | | | | |
| Bank int/charges | | | | | | |
| Total expenditure | | | | | | |
| | | | | | | |
| Balance (+/−) | | | | | | |
| Cumulative | | | | | | |

There are a number of ways of judging how well the salon is doing such as:

● Am I turning away clients?
● Do I have a healthy bank balance?
● Am I busy?
● Am I expanding/growing?

First of all, you need to understand the *calculation of ratios*. The ratio of two figures, e.g. wages to sales, can be expressed in a number of different ways.

Suppose your sales turnover is £50000 and our wages are £30000 then you can say any one of the following:

(1)  The ratio of wages:sales is 30000:50000 or 3:5.
(2)  Wages are 3/5 of sales.
(3)  Wages are 60% of sales.
(4)  $\dfrac{\text{Wages}}{\text{Sales}} = \dfrac{30000}{50000} = 0.6.$
(5)  $\dfrac{\text{Sales}}{\text{Wages}} = \dfrac{50000}{30000} = 1.67\text{x}.$

(6)  Each £ of wages has produced £1.67 of sales.

The standard measure of business performance is *return on capital employed* which is the ratio of net profit before tax to capital employed, i.e.

$$\frac{\text{Net profit before tax}}{\text{Total assets}} \times 100$$

Net profit before tax is obtained from the profit and loss account and total assets is found in the balance sheet. For most businesses, returns of 15–30 per cent are considered good. In hairdressing, because there is a lower investment, especially if premises are rented, returns of 30–120 per cent are possible!

In practice, we can look at two other measures related to sales which are our starting points. These are:

$$\frac{\text{Gross profit}}{\text{Sales}} \times 100$$

and/or

$$\frac{\text{Net profit}}{\text{Sales}} \times 100$$

(Note: Sales or turnover excludes VAT.)

*Gross profit*

This is the difference between sales or turnover (obtained from your profit and loss account) and direct costs, i.e. wages for staff (and you if you cut hair) and consumables, i.e. stock (not retail stock which should be calculated separately), cups of coffee, towels etc. You may need to do some extra calculations to arrive at this figure as most accountants do not present the data clearly in the correct form.

*Example*

| | | | |
|---|---:|---:|---:|
| Turnover excluding VAT | | | £50,000 |
| Wages (including employer's National | | | |
|        Insurance contributions) | | £26,000 | |
| Consumables (excluding VAT) | | £ 2,000 | |
| | | £28,000 | £28,000 |
| | Gross profit | | £22,000 |

Gross profit as a percentage of sales = 44%

$$\left(\text{i.e. } \% = \frac{28000}{50000} \times 100\right).$$

This figure gives you a measure of how well you are controlling your wages and consumable goods. A good hairdressing business must not exceed 53 per cent as a wage cost (including employer's National Insurance contributions) for productive staff, e.g. trainees, receptionists and stylists. If it is significantly less then one of the following areas could be the problem:

(1) Wages are too low and do not provide an incentive to staff to produce more.
(2) The salon owner works harder than any of the staff to pay the stylists' wages.
(3) The staff are being paid cash-in-hand which is illegal.

A good business should achieve 40–50 per cent gross profit. If it is less then you are spending too much on wages and/or consumables. *Consumables will approximately equal stock used* during the year provided you do not have extensive retail sales. *Retail sales should be itemised as a separate stock figure.*

*Net profit*

The second measure is the ratio of net profit before tax to sales/turnover and, again, we examine the percentage value.

$$\text{Net profit \%} = \frac{\text{Net profit before tax}}{\text{Sales (ex VAT)}} \times 100$$

We obtain the net profit figure from our accounts but we must ignore depreciation, i.e. add this back into your reported profit figure. We do this because depreciation is not a real expense, i.e. you do not pay out depreciation, you simply set aside the money to replace assets when they wear out or become out of fashion.

The difference between gross profit and net profit is clearly *expenses* and we would expect a hairdressing business to return between 12 and 20 per cent. If it is lower than this then possibly expenses are too high or your business is not big enough to support them.

The question to be asked is, how well should you be doing? How much profit should you make? Well, apart from as much as possible, you should generate enough to pay the income you want, to earn a reasonable return on the money you have invested and to finance expansion if you wish to expand. The subject of understanding money is covered in much more detail in ISM's *Salon Management Fax Guide* or you could attend one of ISM's Understanding Money courses. We have listed at the back of this book sources of further reading to help with this subject.

## 2.3 How to improve performance

In this section we examine some of the theories behind profit generation and some of the myths, and introduce a new concept – contribution – which is very useful in analysing a hairdressing salon's performance. By now you should be in a position to describe your business in financial terms and to be able to identify the main areas of expense and the way that your profit is generated. You should also be able to calculate the percentage wages, the percentage stock figure, gross profit, expenses and net profit. This

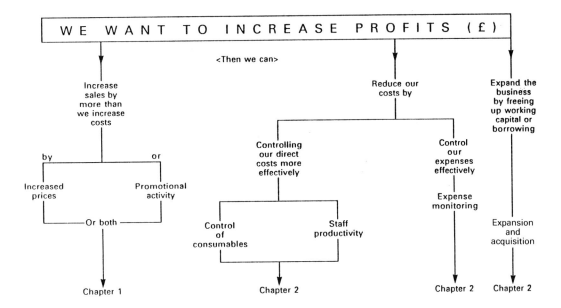

**Fig. 2.4** Ways to increase profits.

information will show you whether the costs are excessive or reasonable. Figure 2.4 shows a model of how to increase profits.

### 2.3.1 Calculating contribution to gross profit

A powerful method for looking at a salon business is to consider the process by which revenue is generated and how costs are incurred and to examine the behaviour of these costs.

*Example*
A client has cut and blow dry and pays £10. In doing so she 'uses up' certain things needed to carry out the treatment:

- Staff payment
- Stock – shampoos, conditioners, perms, finishing aids
- Hot water
- Towels
- Refreshments

Also, of course, she makes use of other things – the overheads – which must be covered in order for the salon to function, e.g. telephone, heating, receptionist costs.

These costs can be split into two distinct categories: those which can be considered as direct and variable costs, i.e. which relate directly to the number of clients and type of service, and those which can be considered as fixed costs, i.e. they do not vary directly with the number of clients.

Cut and blow dry
    Variable costs:
- Wages
- Hot Water/products

- Refreshments

Contribution = Income – Variable costs.

If we carry out the same calculation for all the services we offer then we will have a clearer understanding of contribution to gross profit for each service offered:

| Services | Costs | Contribution | Price (ex VAT) |
|---|---|---|---|
| Cut and blow dry | 3.60 | 2.40 | 6.00 |
| Perm | 2.25 | 1.75 | 4.00 |
| Colouring | 3.50 | 6.50 | 10.00 |
| Retail sales | | 25% | 30.00 per week |

The retail sales figure is (selling price – wholesale cost – commissions) expressed as a percentage of selling price.

From your records you must now estimate or know the volume sales of each service. This should then give you an approximate gross profit figure.

*Example*

| | | |
|---|---|---|
| Cut and blow dry | 40 per week | |
| Shampoo/set | 30 per week | |
| Perm | 8 per week | number of clients |
| Colouring | 6 per week | handled per week |
| Retail sales | £30 per week | |

| Item | Price/unit (£) | Contribution/ unit (£) | Total sales (units) | Total contribution (£) | Total sales (£) |
|---|---|---|---|---|---|
| Cut and blow dry | 6 | 2.40 | 40 | 96.00 | 240 |
| Shampoo/set | 4 | 1.75 | 30 | 52.50 | 120 |
| Perm | 10 | 6.50 | 8 | 52.00 | 80 |
| Colouring | 10 | 6.00 | 6 | 36.00 | 60 |
| Retail sales £30 p.w. × 25% | | | | 7.50 | 30 |
| | | | Totals | 244.00 | 530 |

You should by now be able to understand where your gross profit is coming from – which type of customers and which type of work generate most revenue. It is this understanding of your business that helps you to improve your profit.

If you estimate the time taken for each service then you can calculate contribution per hour of staff time. Suppose we estimate:

| | |
|---|---|
| Cut and blow dry | 30 minutes |
| Shampoo/set | 20 minutes |
| Perm | 1 hour |
| Colouring | 45 minutes |
| Retail sales | 3 minutes per sale (dependent on numbers of clients through the salon per hour) |

(The estimates should be based on time staff actually spend on the service i.e. they cannot do other work, *not* how long the client is in the salon.)

Then our contribution rate per hour is:

Cut and blow dry    $\dfrac{2.40}{30}$  =  8p/minute  =  £4.80 per hour

| | | | | |
|---|---|---|---|---|
| Shampoo/set | $\dfrac{1.75}{20}$ | = 9p/minute | = | £5.40 per hour |
| Perm | $\dfrac{6.50}{60}$ | = 11p/minute | = | £6.60 per hour |
| Colouring | $\dfrac{6.00}{45}$ | = 13p/minute | = | £7.80 per hour |

Retail sales    (Calculations are rounded up or down to the nearest whole penny) based on average sale £1, 25% contribution

So how do we interpret these results? If staff spend one hour doing each of the above then they would generate:

£7.80 per hour for colouring
£6.50 per hour for perming
£5.40 per hour for shampoo/sets
£4.80 per hour for cut and blow dry

So how do your staff spend their time? Where should your greatest effort be? We leave you to see the answers – the facts are clear.

## 2.4 Increasing sales revenue

There are basically two ways of increasing sales revenue – by promotion (including reducing prices) or by raising prices. We will discuss each of these in turn but will concentrate primarily on the second as the first is detailed in section 1.8 Pricing.

Firstly, we must question if there is potential to increase staff productivity. This means calculating how effectively staff use their time. To do this we need to calculate the number of hours worked by staff involved directly in the services to clients, i.e. stylists and trainees.

Suppose we have two full time and two part time staff:

2 full time staff    38 hours each per week × 2 = 76 hours ⎫  Total
2 part time staff  10 hours each per week × 2 = 20 hours ⎬  172 hours
2 trainees           38 hours each per week × 2 = 76 hours ⎭
(don't forget to take off holidays, sick leave and days off)

Now we need to examine the number of hours actually worked on clients. We calculated previously the average time per client per service and by calculating out the services provided:

*Example*

| | | |
|---|---|---|
| 40 cut and blow dries × 30 minutes | = | 1200 minutes |
| 30 shampoo/sets × 20 minutes | = | 600 minutes |
| 8 perms × 60 minutes | = | 480 minutes |
| 8 colourings × 45 minutes | = | 360 minutes |
| 30 retail sales × 3 minutes | = | 90 minutes |
| Total productive time | = | 2,730 minutes or 46 hours |

The productive time ratio is

$$\frac{\text{Productive hours}}{\text{Total hours}} = \frac{46}{172} = 27\%$$

Thus, this salon could potentially increase turnover if its staff were correctly utilised – and this ratio was increased to nearer 100 per cent. In practice, however, it is difficult to improve much past 70 per cent and typically salons achieve 40–55 per cent utilisation. We must remember that a proportion of the salon staff's time will be spent on cleaning, making and serving refreshments, answering the telephone and booking appointments if there is no receptionist, and training staff.

It does draw attention to the need for careful planning of time and spreading clients throughout the day and the week as a whole. You must also question whether you should be employing what will become a rare commodity of young trainees to clean the salon and serve refreshments, particularly as market forces will require salons to pay trainees much higher salaries and develop them in a shorter space of time.

*Raising prices*

We have mentioned raising prices and some hairdressers reading this will say it will drive customers away. If they are customers we do not need then that is good. Let us use an example:

*Example*
Two hairdressers, Michael Idlerich and Tony Graftanbroke, run salons in any town. Both have turnovers of £75 000 per annum. Mike runs a Porsche and Tony a Mini. How? Mike's prices are 57 per cent higher than Tony's and Tony has almost twice as many customers (as you would expect) yet their costs are much the same. We show the analysis in Figure. 2.5.

Mike makes four times as much profit as Tony! Yet he only has half as

| | Cut/blow dry | Shampoo/set | Perms | Retails | Totals | Notes |
|---|---|---|---|---|---|---|
| *Tony Graftanbroke* | | | | | | |
| Price | 11.52 | 9.00 | 23.00 | 3.00 | | |
| No. of clients | 80 | 50 | 5 | 10 | 145 | Per week |
| Weekly turnover | 922.00 | 450.00 | 115.00 | 30.00 | 1,517 | £75,850* |
| Direct costs/unit | 10.36 | 6.00 | 10.00 | 2.00 | | As we estimated earlier |
| Contribution unit | 1.16 | 3.00 | 13.00 | 1.00 | per unit | |
| Gross profit/ week | 93.00 | 150.00 | 65.00 | 10.00 | 318.00 | £15,900* |
| Expenses | | | | | | £8,640 |
| Profit | | | | | | £7,260 p.a. |
| *Michael Idlerich* | | | | | | |
| Price | 18.72 | 13.00 | 35.00 | 14.00 | | |
| No. of clients | 50 | 25 | 5 | 5 | 85 | Per week |
| Weekly turnover | 936.00 | 325.00 | 175.00 | 70.00 | 1,506 | £75,300* |
| Direct costs/unit | 10.36 | 6.00 | 10.00 | 9.00 | | |
| Contribution/unit | 8.36 | 7.00 | 25.00 | 5.00 | – | |
| Gross profit/ week | 418.00 | 175.00 | 125.00 | 25.00 | 743 | £37,150* |
| Expenses | | | | | | £8,640 |
| Profit | | | | | | £28,510 |

* calculated on a 50 week trading year

**Fig. 2.5** Comparison of two salons.

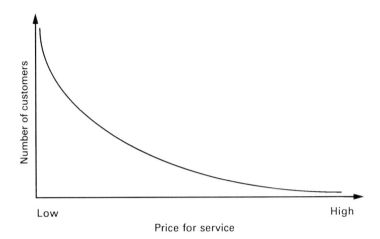

**Fig. 2.6** Price demand curve.

many clients. Mike has realised by analysing contribution he is better off by having fewer clients paying more per person than dozens paying less. This is the basic law of profit. You allow your prices to drift to the level at which profit is maximised. Figure 2.6 shows you the theory. For any given price there is an associated demand. If the price is very high you will have too few customers. Too low and you will be swamped. If you calculate your contribution versus price curve it will look like Fig. 2.7.

What this analysis shows is that raising prices and losing customers is not necessarily a bad thing. A major problem for the industry is that prices are generally too low and thus competition revolves around price. If you *selectively* raise prices, e.g. on busy days, this will improve staff utilisation by moving some customers to other days and will prevent clients from being turned away; then you have the key to keeping clients at prices that will make your business profitable. This in turn means more time for the salon owner or manager to manage instead of running around in circles. More time on planning, promotions and managing our businesses profitably. The concept of pricing can be used to:

- Raise prices on busy days and times
- Lower prices on quiet days and times

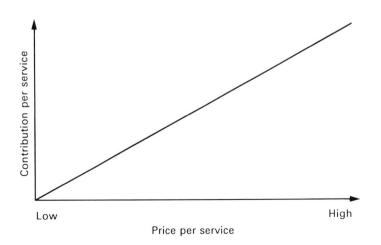

**Fig. 2.7** Contribution versus price curve.

This achieves both of our goals which are to:

(1) raise total contribution
(2) increase staff productivity by increasing throughput

## 2.5 Controlling direct costs

In the previous section we aimed to increase your gross profit by improving productivity and raising or reducing prices. In this section we examine how to monitor and control your direct costs and try to improve your performance of them.

First of all you need to ask yourselves the following questions:

(1) Have my direct costs gone up, down or remained the same over the last six months, year or two years?
(2) How do my costs compare with the competition?
(3) Do I pay my staff more, the same, or less for the equivalent work than my competitors?
(4) Do I manage my stock properly?

The answers to these questions lie at the heart of effective gross profit management.

Let us first of all examine *consumables*. From your records let us look at the value of your stock. You need to separate out the stock for retail sales and the stocks of products used in producing the service.

Carrying excess stock is a serious problem for hairdressers. Imagine you cannot buy more products at all: how long would your stock last? One week, month, year? Ideally, you should carry as little as possible, i.e. one week–one month at the most. Yet we have found hairdressers carrying over a year's stock – usually because they wish to go on an overseas seminar provided by a manufacturer! So why is too much stock bad news? Here are some reasons:

(1) Stock is money tied up (this is particularly important if your business runs on a bank loan).
(2) Excessive stock causes waste because staff use more and throw away more.
(3) Excessive stock gets damaged.
(4) Stock goes off and becomes obsolete, especially colours.
(5) Excessive stock gets stolen.

The second aspect of stock is getting it at the right price. If you buy in large catering or bulk packs and wish to avoid waste ensure you issue stock in small quantities to avoid unnecessary waste, such as using shampoo dispensers etc. This way you can get the benefit of bulk. A stock room or at least a lockable cupboard can keep it safe when not needed. Put a member of staff in charge of noting when things get low and reminding you to re-order and ensure that you have a staff purchase record book to control staff usage at home.

Stock, however, is likely to be a relatively small cost compared to staff costs. These can account for anything between 50 and 80 per cent of all costs of the business. Are your staff productive and do you use them effectively? If you have done the calculations in the previous section you will have some idea as to how well you utilise the staff. As we have mentioned in the previous sections, we do not believe in back-door payment methods or underpaying staff. A payment system should ensure that staff get a reasonable level of pay for a given level of work and should also motivate them to work efficiently without lowering standards. This is important if you are to retain staff in the business and to keep costs under reasonable control.

An analysis that is helpful in this area is the turnover–contribution–wages analysis. Many systems of pay are straight commission, e.g. 50 per cent, and these have disadvantages in that they understate the contribution made to the business. The problem with straight commission schemes is that as the productivity rises the wage costs rise in proportion to productivity. This creates 'a bottoming-out effect' as stylists can only generate so many clients and so much work per day *unless they concentrate their energies on selling more services that generate a higher contribution to gross profit, e.g. colours and retail sales.* This is where technical skills training, speed training and your pricing strategy are essential in increasing productivity and reducing wage costs.

Let us examine these approaches in more detail. Salons could weight the prices of certain services more heavily so as to encourage staff to work harder to sell certain types of product.

Another low cost way of increasing staff salaries and reducing wage percentages is by encouraging retail sales. We are amazed that the enormous retail market for hair care and beauty products is so small in the hairdressing industry. Recent market research shows that 1.25 per cent is the national average for retail sales in hairdressing salons yet the market is worth £488 million. We believe the key to retail selling is as follows:

- Retail sales training of staff
- A good display area
- Products displayed at styling positions
- Incentive schemes to generate sales
- Staff understanding *why* retail sales are part of the service to be offered to a client

A further analysis is to examine how much work each member of staff brings in – preferably work on contribution not turnover and examine which staff are low and why. Salons frequently have poor book procedures which leave some stylists exhausted and others bored. It is better to encourage clients to change stylists within the salon than to lose them. Why is it that often older stylists receive all the shampoo/blow dries or shampoo and sets which are traditionally priced at a lower rate than cuts and finishes? By the pay scheme and price structure that are traditionally in force in the industry we are penalising older stylists for taking older clients who, traditionally, have blow dries and shampoo and sets at a lower price. It is not surprising, therefore, that they become bored and demotivated. An interesting exercise to adopt in a salon would be to ask staff the following question:

> Imagine you had to pay all staff £200 per week including trainees and you could not sack anybody. How would you do things differently?

Another approach, which some salon owners find profitable, is the use of good part-time staff, especially married women or women returners. These will be people who may not necessarily wish to work long hours or every day but if the hours and pay were right would willingly work. In fact, these are often mobile or home hairdressers who work on the side but who, if properly channelled, could produce good work for you rather than against you.

In conclusion, you need to carefully analyse your staff costs, productivity and the payment system to ensure that they meet the criteria we set earlier. You must:

- Control your costs effectively
- Motivate staff
- Guarantee reasonable income levels for all
- Utilise a system that is easy to understand and administer
- Utilise a system that is credible to staff
- Be competitive in your locality to avoid losing your best staff to competition

## 2.6 Controlling expenses

In previous sections we have looked at increasing productivity and controlling direct costs. In this section we examine the nature of expenses and ways of systematically reducing them. It should not need to be emphasised that every pound saved is a pound extra profit. The same principles apply as to all other items:

- Where exactly is the expense?
- Is it necessary?
- Can we get the item cheaper?
- Are we spending more than last year?
- Are we spending more than competition?

Bear in mind the following commonly used quotes:

'Every business overspends and does not control costs.'
'The man who thinks he is efficient is on the way to insolvency.'

### 2.6.1 General guidelines

(1) Whenever purchasing any item over £50 always get three quotes and choose the middle one.
(2) Avoid credit if you have cash.
(3) Always ask for discounts – even solicitors' and accountants' fees are negotiable.
(4) If you feel over-charged, pay what you think the job is worth and invite them to sue for the rest.
(5) Keep your eyes open for ways of saving money. Have a staff suggestion scheme and give prizes for ideas.

### 2.6.2 Salon operating expenses

*Rent*

(1) See if it is negotiable.
(2) Have you spare space? Can you let it without interfering with your business?
(3) Can you get a discount for payment in advance?

*Rates*

(1) Are there any grounds for a rate reduction (leaflets from your local council)?
(2) Is there any discount for paying in advance? Probably not, so pay by instalments if there is no penalty.

*Water*

(1) As Rates above.

*Repairs/renewals*

(1) Can you do any yourself? Or can the staff?
(2) Any OAPs/handymen locally (cheaper than builders)?
(3) Are you buying fittings etc. at trade discounts? Find a customer whose husband is in the trade.

*Light and heat*

(1) Is your lighting efficient and adequately planned? Is it timed properly, e.g. time switches?
(2) Bulbs etc. Can you buy them at trade prices?
(3) Is your heat insulation adequate?
(4) Is your equipment modern and efficient?
(5) Do you use off-peak electricity?
(6) Avoid leaving heaters on.
(7) Install a double-door to reduce heat losses.

*Insurances*

(1) Have you shopped around (not just a 'friend of the family'!)?
(2) Have you insured for exactly what you want?
(3) Consider different companies for different things.
(4) Can you get discounts?

*Cleaning*

(1) As in Repairs/renewals.
(2) Consider possible investment in equipment.

### 2.6.3 Salon administration

*Telephone*

(1) Have you a call-box for staff?
(2) Monitor for yourself (or buy a British Telecom kit).
(3) Avoid using the telephone before 1.00 pm.
(4) Don't wait – get them to ring you back.
(5) If it's non-urgent, use a letter!
(6) Avoid long distances/overseas calls.

*Accountancy/audit*

(1)  Shop around carefully.
(2)  Ask for breakdown of costs.
(3)  Keep books yourself properly and reduce work.
(4)  Use him effectively – he will save you his fee. Fire him if he can't!

*Stationery/postage*

(1)  Use second class always.
(2)  Use scrap paper – both sides.
(3)  Shop around for printing.
(4)  Use two qualities – image/non-image.
(5)  Re-use envelopes – non-image.
(6)  Ask for cheapest methods at the Post Office (parcels and mail shots).

*Advertising/promotion*

This is a hard area on which to give definite rules but Chapter 1 Marketing and promotions gives some special low cost methods of promotion. The general guidelines are:

(1)  Shop around
(2)  Measure cost-effectiveness
(3)  Use manufacturers' specialist resources – they want your business, e.g. to buy their products, and in return it is often better to negotiate a lower discount but with specialised promotional, technical and management training support instead.

This is the area which can bankrupt you. Manufacturers' resources can be a low cost method.

### 2.6.4 Motor vehicle costs

*Running expenses*

(1)  Shop around for insurance.
(2)  Use small local garages not *main dealers*!
(3)  Avoid obscure cars.
(4)  Buy parts trade.
(5)  Do it yourself.
(6)  Buy oil from discount stores.

*Leasing/hire cost*

(1)  Is it worth leasing? (Ask your accountant.)
(2)  Use cash or HP at 0% finance?
(3)  Ask for discount.
(4)  Import (new cars only).

### 2.6.5 Financial costs

(1)  Use as few accounts as possible.

(2)  Do not keep money in deposit or current accounts except to avoid bank charges.
(3)  Use a building society.
(4)  Read *Money Which*.
(5)  Change banks to the best one for you (it depends on savings or borrowings).
(6)  If possible, increase your mortgage rather than get a bank loan to finance your business.
(7)  Avoid bank charges – ask about 'trigger' accounts.
(8)  Use your financial adviser for advice!

If you review the above points regularly about your business you will be surprised at how much you can save.

## 2.7 Acquiring or selling a business

There are a number of considerations involved in buying or selling a business, both financial and non-financial, and in this section we examine the methods available for putting a value on the business in purely financial terms. The other factors are outside the scope of this book but we have detailed some further reading on this subject. An alternative approach to acquiring a business would be franchising – a growth business within the UK and Europe which we predict will continue to grow during the remainder of this decade. In Chapter 10 The future of the hairdressing industry I give my thoughts and views on franchising.

In this section we will look at the valuation of business in the purely financial sense. When any business is purchased you purchase two aspects:

(1)  The assets of the business less any liabilities or outstanding debts.
(2)  The ability to earn future profits or future earnings – sometimes called the 'goodwill' of the business.

(Note: Goodwill in accounting terms is measured as the difference between the price paid for the business and the above two items)

In the worst case we consider buying an unsuccessful business or one where there is considerable doubt as to future profits. In this case you should pay only the market value of the assets, i.e. what they would realise if sold separately, such as equipment or styling chairs. Whether we value these at crisis sale (sale at gunpoint!) or sale without duress is open to question. The starting point would still be the balance sheet.

Balance sheet of Graftanbroke

| Assets | | £ |
|---|---|---|
| Property (at cost) | | 15,000 |
| Fixtures/fittings | | 5,000 |
| Stock | | 1,200 |
| Cash | | 500 |
| | Assets | 21,700 |
| | Creditors | 700 |
| | Net valuation | 21,000 |

Unfortunately, balance sheets tend to show historical figures and some assets, especially property, may need to be valued upwards, whereas other items, especially if sold under duress, may go down sharply, especially stock and fixtures. Therefore, revaluation in the light of market conditions may be:

| *Assets* | | £ |
|---|---|---|
| Property (current value) | | 17,000 |
| Fixtures (market value) | | 2,000 |
| Stock (market value) | | 500 |
| Cash | | 500 |
| | Assets | 20,000 |
| | Creditors | 700 |
| | | 19,300 |

Under these conditions, £19300 would be a better price to pay.

In practice, we normally buy a business as a going concern, i.e. with a history and a future of profits. In this case we may have a number of methods available to us.

Hairsense

| *Balance sheet* | | (revalued as before) |
|---|---|---|
| *Assets* | | £ |
| Buildings | | 20,000 |
| Vehicles | | 2,000 |
| Fixtures/fittings | | 2,500 |
| Stock | | 1,000 |
| | Assets | 25,500 |
| | Creditors | 500 |
| | | 25,000 |

*Profits 1977–1981*

| 1977 | £ 9,000 |
|---|---|
| 1978 | £10,000 |
| 1979 | £12,000 |
| 1980 | £13,000 |
| 1981 | £15,000 |

We value this company in two stages. Firstly, if we assume a reasonable rate of return for this type of business is 15 per cent, then a reasonable profit would be 15 per cent of £25000, i.e. £3750. Thus the excess profits (called super profits) were:

| 1977 | £ 5,000 |
|---|---|
| 1978 | £ 6,000 |
| 1979 | £ 8,000 |
| 1980 | £ 9,000 |
| 1981 | £11,000 |

It is for these superprofits that we will pay goodwill and two methods of valuation are common:

(1)  Purchase × years, e.g. last 3 years, i.e. £28000 or 3 × last year, i.e. £33000. This would value the business at either £25000 + £28000 = £53000, or £58000.

(2)  Capitalise profits at higher rate, say 25 per cent (because they are riskier), thus take the average figure for the last 3 years, i.e. £9000 and

multiply by 4 = £36000. On this basis the valuation is £25000 + £36000 – £61000

Note: capitalisation

| Rate | Factor |
|------|--------|
| 10% | 10 |
| 15% | 7 |
| 20% | 5 |
| 25% | 4 |
| 33% | 3 |
| 50% | 2 |

i.e. $\text{Factor} = \dfrac{100\%}{\text{Capital rate (\%)}}$

So we see that this valuation offers a range of £53000 – £61000. It is in this area that we would negotiate.

Another method sometimes used is to choose a suitable capitalisation rate and capitalise all profits.

*Example*
If we decided a rate of 20 per cent here then we would value the business at 5 × recent profits:

$$5 \times 11000 = £55000$$

Notice all methods give a similar result.

The choice of capitalisation rate is dependent upon:

- Rates of interest available for money
- Plus risk allowance (the riskier the business the higher the rate): 20–30 per cent seem appropriate rates at the present time for hairdressing businesses

In conclusion, there are more complex issues involved. Buying into a share of a business, a partnership or public quoted company is outside the scope of this book but the principles are similar. In this section we have argued that the business must be seen as a financial vehicle taking in cash and producing cash and that we must examine ways of increasing profit by:

(1) Increasing revenue
(2) Reducing direct costs (increasing gross profit)
(3) Decreasing expenses

We have emphasised the need for monitoring performance and keeping records to analyse potential areas for profit improvement by the use of contribution analysis. We examined this concept in relationship to staff productivity and pricing and showed its effects on staff motivation by relating it to wage costs. We also looked at methods of reducing expenses and examined briefly how to value a business for sale or purchasing purposes.

# Chapter Three
# Finding staff and keeping them

## 3.1 Introduction

Recruitment and selection begin with the notification by a member of staff that they are leaving, or the opening of a new salon, or the decision to employ additional members of staff. They end with the arrival of the new staff member, his/her induction and, where used, the satisfactory completion of a probationary period.

One of the things which untrained people are surprised at is how much work there is before the interview. It is not simply a case of advertise – pull them in – pick them (and sack them if they are no good!). In selection one needs to adopt the role of a detective, collecting facts, sifting evidence, coming to logical conclusions and learning by experience. These are the key skills involved in recruiting and selecting staff effectively.

If we adopt an analytical approach to these procedures of selection and make the integration of that new staff member as smoothly and quickly as possible into our salons then we will have much greater success in keeping that new staff member employed for a number of years.

In the hairdressing industry the turnover of new trainees is at its highest within the first three months of employing them. Why is this? Is it because we do not take time to select staff correctly? Is it that we see selection of staff as a one way process – the salon decides who they will employ? In reality the selection of staff for a new job is always a two-way process. This may surprise you. The salon must make the job as attractive as possible but must also point out the pitfalls. The salon must also select the correct person for the job by comparing facts about the potential candidates as opposed to selecting staff on gut-feeling, instinct or the 'I can pick them as soon as they walk through the door' approach. The potential new staff member selects whether they wish to work for your salon depending upon how it is packaged.

Many of you, as you read this chapter, will have begun to realise the shortage of school leavers and the potential problems this will have for the hairdressing industry. In fact, the shortage of school leavers will continue to blight the industry until the end of the century. But we can turn this apparent problem to one of advantage by seriously looking at the way in which we select staff, the way in which we train and develop them, the type of employment package we offer to staff to attract them and the various incentives that can be used to ensure that they continue to stay with us.

Later on in this chapter I have detailed potential ways in which we could rethink the whole way we approach employing apprentices and young people within the hairdressing industry.

## 3.2 Analysing the job

We can distinguish between recruitment and selection in that *recruitment* is concerned with producing a field of potential candidates and *selection* is the choice process between them. Many activities are clearly common and we will label these as both recruitment and selection.

Whenever and wherever vacancies occur, this should be an opportunity to rethink staffing issues:

- Are we over/under-staffed?
- Do we lack certain skills that we need?
- Do we need an exact copy of the person who left or not?

These are the sort of questions that need to be considered before making any further move towards recruiting more staff. This clearly requires consideration of the current workload and the current staff levels and their skills in order to identify exactly what is needed.

The two key questions to ask are:

(1)  Why has the vacancy occurred?
(2)  What skills are needed to fill the vacancy?

*Why has the vacancy occurred?*

Check the following list:

(1)  Member of staff leaving due to:

  - Another job
  - Moving from the area
  - Pregnancy

(2)  Promotion
(3)  Ill health
(4)  New skills required, e.g. tinting, long hair work, training skills, photographic skills
(5)  Salon expansion

Asking the above question helps us to identify if there is a pattern in our business as to why staff may be leaving which may affect our future approach to recruiting staff.

If you have, however, decided to go ahead and recruit, then consider recruitment as consisting of a number of stages:

(1)  Job description – defining the job, its responsibilities and levels of authority
(2)  Person specification – defining the person and skills required to fill the job
(3)  Attracting a field of candidates
(4)  Selecting the staff
(5)  Incorporating the staff into the organisation

If we look at the flow chart shown in Fig. 3.1 we will see a very clear stage by stage process which is necessary in the recruitment/selection process.

Now complete Exercise 3.1. This will give you a measure of how much work needs to be put into practice in order to make recruitment/selection an effective process.

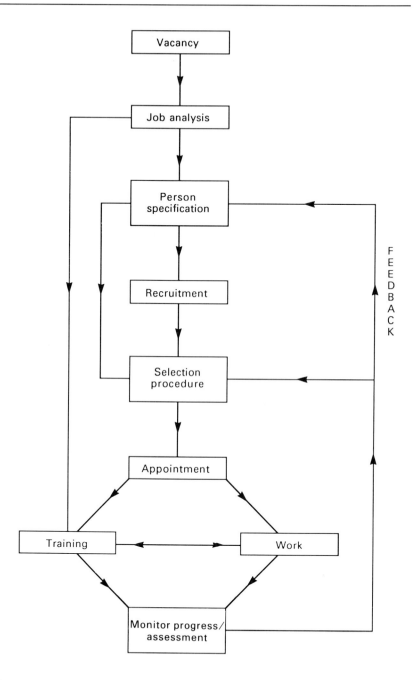

**Fig. 3.1** A model of recruitment/selection process.

**Exercise 3.1 Recruitment/selection**
Answer TRUE or FALSE to each statement.

(1) All my staff have written job descriptions. _____

(2) I use job descriptions when I interview new staff. _____

(3) I prepare person specifications for each interview. _____

(4) I interview in a quiet room free from interruptions. _____

(5) I always take up basic references for staff. _____

(6) I always prepare an interview plan before I interview
for new staff. _____

(7) I have never picked a bad member of staff. _____

(8) I always tell staff about the bad parts of the job as well
as the good. _____

(9) I always get my receptionist or senior stylist or
another stylist to 'look after' a new member of staff. _____

(10) I always sit down and talk to a new staff member a
short time after they've joined to discuss progress and
problems. _____

*Scoring*
Score 1 for all TRUE answers except for (7) score –2 (everybody makes mistakes). Score 0 for all FALSE answers.

*Score interpretation*
Less than 2   You are either lucky or unsuccessful in the way you select staff.
2–5   You have still a lot to learn about successful staff selection.
More than 7   Excellent. You are well on the way to success.

## 3.3 The job description

A job description is a statement of the overall purpose of the job and the main tasks to be carried out. A good job description is essential to effective selection but it is also relevant to all the other processes by which we manage our staff. It is a vital document which notes what the staff are actually doing.

*Purposes of a job description:*

- Motivation of staff
- Staff appraisal/monitoring their progress
- Disciplining staff and handling staff problems
- Training staff
- Man-power planning
- Part of their contract of employment

A good job description should contain the following items:

(1) Location of job
(2) Job title

(3) Job title of immediate superior/supervisor
(4) Job grade (if relevant)
(5) Job titles of any staff for whom the job holder is responsible (numbers)
(6) Brief description of overall purpose of the job
(7) The main tasks to be carried out by the job holder listed preferably in order of importance
(8) The standards required from the job holder
(9) Details of any special requirements, e.g. supplying of equipment, travelling or outside visiting etc.
(10) Special circumstances of job, e.g. hours, overtime (evening) or weekend working, unpleasant conditions etc.

Sample job descriptions for a stylist and salon manager are shown. These are examples and not intended as perfect specimens. The needs of each salon are different and general job descriptions are of little use – they must reflect the actual job as it is required to be done.

---

**Job description**

Job title:                     Stylist
Location:
Main purpose of job:           To ensure that the standards of the Company are reached and maintained under the following key categories:

- Financial/productivity standards
- Hairdressing standards
- Service standards
- Image/appearance standards
- Behaviour standards
- Salon procedures.

Responsible to:                The Salon Manager and, in the absence of the Manager, the Assistant Manager.
Responsibilities:

*Financial/productivity standards*
(1) To achieve a realistic pre-set target of takings
(2) To ensure that daily/weekly worksheets balance with the takings
(3) To ensure that retail sales figures are recorded accurately and balance
(4) To ensure maximum use is gained from the appointments system
(5) To ensure all services provided are charged for at the correct current price list

*Hairdressing standards*
(1) To achieve and maintain hairdressing standards and techniques in keeping with the clients' wishes and current fashion trends.
(2) To take fullest advantage and use of all training available within the Company.
(3) To assist in the training and to encourage all trainees in the practical application of hairdressing skills and service standards.

*Service standards*
(1) To advise clients of all services and products available and, in particular, those for retail purchase in order that they keep their hair in good condition.

(2) To ensure clients are offered and are aware of all non-hairdressing services available, e.g. coffee/tea, magazines etc., in order to ensure client comfort.
(3) To maintain and update client record cards for the following reasons:

- Technical
- Client complaints

*Image/appearance standards*
(1) To ensure your personal appearance is in keeping with the standards set by Management with regard to staff dress, hairstyles, make-up and personal hygiene as set out in the Company's Rules and Regulations.
(2) To ensure that salon cleanliness and hygiene is maintained and in keeping with the Company's policy in services.
(3) To work with the Manager in promoting the Company's image through all media, e.g. advertising, shows (trade and public) and local publicity to increase the Company's reputation and client count.

*Behaviour standards*
(1) To adhere to the Company's policy on staff behaviour as set out in the Company's Rules and Regulations, e.g. hours of work etc.
(2) To be loyal to other members of staff and management at all times.
(3) To ensure a friendly and approachable attitude towards clients is maintained at all times.
(4) To be aware of the grievance procedure and to ensure it is carried out as laid down in the individual's Contract of Employment.

*Salon procedures*
(1) To carry out all reasonable duties and tasks which may be requested of you.

---

**Job description**

Job title: Salon Manager
Location:
Main purpose of job: Responsibility for the efficient running and profitability of the salon by ensuring that the standards of the Company are reached and maintained under the following key categories:

- Financial/productivity standards
- Hairdressing standards
- Service standards
- Staff management standards
- Image/appearance standards
- Salon procedures

Responsible to: General Manager with a close direct working relationship with Training Manager

Responsibilities:

*Financial/productivity standards*
(1) To adhere to the financial guidelines as follows:

- To achieve quarterly financial/service mix targets for the salon
- To ensure staff offer a full range of services that the salon has available
- To ensure the smooth running of reception area, in particular with overall responsibility for cash and paperwork procedures

- To ensure all services provided are charged for at the correct current price
- To ensure daily takings and float balance with work carried out
- To ensure correct information is recorded by staff on daily/weekly worksheets

(2) To achieve a realistic pre-set target of promotional activities as and when they occur.
(3) To ensure the ordering and maintaining of stock levels are carried out according to the guidelines set by the General Manager and that paperwork procedures are completed accurately.
(4) To ensure that reception and bill procedures are completed accurately according to the Company policy currently in force.

*Hairdressing standards*
(1) In conjunction with the Training Manager to organise and put into action a full training programme for junior staff to ensure that the required standard of proficiency is reached within the required time.
(2) To work with the Training Manager in maintaining hairdressing standards and techniques in keeping with clients' wishes and current fashion trends.

*Service standards*
(1) To maintain and constantly review client service standards.
(2) To advise clients of all services and products available and, in particular, those for retail purchase in order that they keep their hair in good condition.
(3) To ensure that staff update and maintain client record cards for the following reasons:

- Technical
- Client complaints

(4) To ensure the salon has sufficient stock in order that sales and services are not inhibited.

*Staff management*
(1) To motivate and guide all members of staff to create a happy working atmosphere for the benefit of both staff and clients, e.g. working hours are adhered to etc.
(2) To encourage and motivate all staff to maximum potential, both technically and professionally, for their individual benefit and the future growth of the Company.
(3) To communicate through all staff levels, i.e. stylists, trainees, receptionist, the following information:

- Company policies and procedures
- Staff changes
- The Company's future plans
- Management satisfaction and dissatisfaction
- Feed-back through correct channels on staff criticisms, ensuring that these are given a satisfactory answer

(4) To ensure that grievance procedures are carried out as laid down in the individual's Contract of Employment.
(5) Together with the General Manager to plan future staff requirements to maintain staff levels with fluctuations in trade throughout the year.
(6) To plan a holiday rota for staff ensuring that only one stylist is absent at any one time and to take into account the salon's needs regarding busy periods.

(7) To carry out first interviews to find suitable candidates before final selection is made by the General Manager and/or Training Manager (dependant upon the level of the job).

*Image/appearance standards*

(1) To ensure that staff's appearance is in keeping with the standards set by management with regard to staff dress, hairstyles, make-up and personal hygiene as set out in the Company's Rules and Regulations.
(2) To ensure salon cleanliness and maintenance is in keeping with the Company's policy on services.
(3) To ensure that there are suitable merchandising displays for both salon services and retail products.
(4) To work closely with the General Manager in promoting the Company's image through all media, i.e. advertising, shows (trade and public) and local publicity to increase the Company's reputation and client count.

*Salon procedures*

(1) To ensure the salon is secure at all times and, in particular, with regard to cash/financial procedures.
(2) To ensure that the systems and procedures which may be in force at any time are adhered to.
(3) To carry out all reasonable duties and tasks which may be requested.

---

So how do you go about writing a job description? There are a number of options:

(1) Sit down and write up the job as you see it.
(2) Ask the person doing the job to produce a synopsis as they see it.
(3) Interview the job holder about what he/she actually does.
(4) Get him/her to keep a detailed log or record (diary) of his/her activities.
(5) Get a consultant to do it for you.
(6) Any combination of the above or *all* if you wish.

The important thing to bear in mind is that the aim of the exercise is to produce the best possible job description available in the time.

*Standards*

What must be included in a job description is the approach to the standards required. There are five main standards within the hairdressing industry:

(1) Standards of hairdressing
(2) Standards of appearance
(3) Standards of productivity
(4) Standards of service
(5) Standards of behaviour

Figures 3.2–3.6 show flow charts of the areas in which, in our opinion, standards should be measured within the hairdressing industry. Without standards how is it possible to have any level of professionalism? These standards must be:

● Definable
● Measurable
● Achievable

**Fig. 3.2** Setting
standards of
hairdressing.

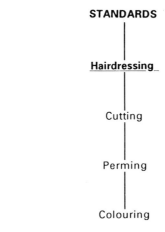

**Fig. 3.3** Setting
standards of
appearance.

**Fig. 3.4** Setting
standards of
productivity.

**Fig. 3.5** Setting standards of service.

**STANDARDS**

**Service**

Clients
not kept waiting

Coffee/magazines

Hair happy

Hair care advice

**Fig. 3.6** Setting standards of behaviour.

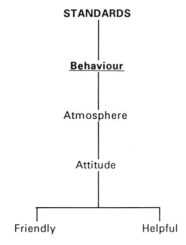

**STANDARDS**

**Behaviour**

Atmosphere

Attitude

Friendly          Helpful

Each salon will have different standards, for example, of hairdressing and service depending upon their client mix, the area in which the salon is situated and all the other factors discussed in Chapter 1 Marketing and promotions.

Finally, if you already have a job description with all the things detailed as previously discussed, it is important to revise it:

- Regularly
- Whenever it changes

**Fig. 3.7** Person
specification form.

| Characteristics | Minimum requirement | Desirable requirement |
|---|---|---|
| (1) Physique, health and appearance<br>• Height and build<br>• Hearing and eyesight<br>• Looks, grooming, dress/clothes<br>• Voice and personal manner<br>• General health/fitness | | |
| (2) Education and previous experience<br>• Education level – GCSE,'O', 'A' Level<br>• Specific training, apprenticeship, professional training<br>• Job training<br>• Experience required, number of years/type required | | |
| (3) Intelligence level | | |
| (4) Special talents<br>• Does the job involve practical things?<br>• Skill with writing reports and communicating with clients/staff<br>• Skill with figures or handling money<br>• Artistic flair/ability e.g. dressing hair, stagework, photographic experience<br>• Using tools or special equipment | | |
| (5) Personal interests<br>• Active or outdoor<br>• Intellectual/logical<br>• Practical<br>• Artistic<br>• Social – persuading, managing, entertaining people | | |
| (6) Temperament<br>• Acceptability to others<br>• Leadership/influencing<br>• Stability/steadiness<br>• Self-reliance (working alone and accepting responsibility)<br>• Ability to handle stress | | |
| (7) Personal circumstances<br>• Married/single<br>• Dependents<br>• Age preference<br>• Travel requirements | | |

A vacancy gives you a natural opportunity to check out whether the current job description is still valid, and if not, to correct it.

## 3.4 Identifying the right person

Now that a description of the exact nature of the job has been produced, the next stage is to analyse the qualities of the person required to fill the job. This is the stage which requires human judgement and there is no real alternative. There are a number of check lists which help you to achieve this and we will use Alec Rodger's *Seven Point Plan* which identifies seven aspects of the individual which are:

- Physique
- Attainment
- General intelligence
- Special aptitudes
- Interests
- Disposition
- Circumstances

Figure 3.7 shows a person specification form which has been designed for use in the hairdressing business. Try to complete it for a job of your choice. In doing this bear in mind two questions:

(1) What is absolutely *essential* for reasonable performance of the job?
(2) What is *desirable* or *preferable* in a candidate if you have a choice?

These are recorded in the 'minimum' and 'desirable' requirement columns of the person specification and must be quantified wherever possible and written in a way which indicates how they will be measured. Figure 3.8 indicates some of the key aspects we would include in a person specification for a stylist.

*Points to remember*

(1) The person specification should not be simply a copy of the last job holder but should be considered in relation to the current job.
(2) Beware of asking too much – remember if you over-specify or your standards are too high, you will find it difficult to recruit anyone at all.
(3) Be as clear as possible – imagine you had to give this form to someone else to do the interview for you.

**Fig. 3.8** Key qualities of a stylist.

(1) Attractive appearance
(2) Fashionable clothes
(3) Outgoing personality – 'bubbly'
(4) Artistic flair
(5) Proper professional training
(6) Ability to relate to clients
(7) Social skills
(8) Energy and stamina

(4) Try to be objective and avoid your own prejudices/biases. Try to match each feature back to the job requirements.
(5) Try to note which requirements could be achieved by training and which cannot be changed in the potential candidate. For example, selling skills may be desirable but not essential, people can be trained in selling! People can be trained in advanced colouring techniques.
(6) Aim to produce a clear mental picture of the person you want to fill the job. This framework can be used for shortlisting and selection.

## 3.5 Analysing the person

The following points can be considered under the various headings:

(1) Physique, health and appearance

- Standard of health/fitness required
- Importance of first impressions (appearance, speech etc.)
- Social skills and experience
- Clothes sense

(2) Education and previous experience
What knowledge and/or experience does the person need?

- General education – 'O' level, 'A' level etc
- Specific training, apprenticeships (was it a traditional apprenticeship; through a college of FE; or a private school), professional qualifications, job training
- Experience required. Number of years/type required

(3) Special talents

- Does the job involve practical things (working with the hands)?
- Does it involve writing reports or communication with clients/staff?
- Does it involve calculating, figurework or handling money?
- How much artistic flair/ability is needed? For example dressing hair, stagework, photographic experience
- Does it involve using tools or special equipment?

(4) Intelligence
Most difficult to estimate – above or below or about average?

(5) Personal interests
Interests are often a guide to a person's personality and preferences. Beware of people with too many interests! What interests does the job appeal to?

- Active or outdoor interests
- Intellectual or logical
- Practical
- Artistic
- Social – persuading managing, entertaining people

(6) Temperament
What sort of person is required to do the job?

- Acceptability to others
- Leadership or influencing

- Stability and steadiness
- Self reliance (working alone and accepting responsibility)
- Ability to handle stress

(7) Personal circumstances
Any personal circumstances relevant to job, e.g. married/single, dependents, age preference, travel requirements etc.

Now using the person specification form shown in Fig. 3.7 prepare a person specification for the job of a stylist or trainee. Once you have done this a clearer picture can be formed as to the type of person required to fill the position.

## 3.6 Attracting potential candidates

Now you have done your homework on the person you are looking for you can decide from where to recruit them. There are a large number of places to recruit staff from and Fig. 3.9 lists them, notes the advantages and disadvantages of each and suggests what they might be useful for. Notice that some of the methods are free or at least inexpensive. Most hairdressers fail to use all the options open to them.

If you use a method which requires an advert then you will need to design this in an effective way. We provide in section 3.6.1 a guide to writing job adverts. You must be careful to avoid infringing the Sex Discrimination Act (1975) and Fig. 9.1 summarises the main points as they apply to hairdressers. The Equal Opportunities Commission provides a free booklet on this area (see further sources at the back of the book).

### 3.6.1 A guide to writing job advertisements

The points in these guidelines apply to all advertisements.
The aims of recruitment advertising are:

(1) *Reach* the target audience.

(2) *Attract* and *retain* attention.

(3) Produce a *compact* field of acceptable candidates who are:

- capable/equipped to do the job
- motivated to apply for it
- motivated to actually *do* the job if successful

It is fallacy that a large number of applicants means a good advert.

(4) The contents of the advert should be:

- *concise*
- *factual*
- *relevant* to the job, the applicant and method of recruitment
- *unambiguous*

(5) Ideally the advert should contain:

- The *job title*, or an easily understood phrase to help convey the job
- The *rewards* (salary and relevant fringe benefits)
- The *location(s)*

**Fig. 3.9** Methods
of recruitment.

| Method | Advantages | Disadvantages | Use for |
|---|---|---|---|
| Previous staff | You know them. Low cost | Does not introduce new ideas | Any |
| Previous applicants | Low cost | May not be interested | Any |
| Personal recommendations (Clients/staff/friends) | Low cost. Can get good information | May not be reliable information. Difficulties if unsuitable | Any |
| Direct mailing | Low cost. Can be lucky | Hit and miss method | Any Combine with a promotion |
| Schools (Careers Officer) | Low cost. Can get good choice of students | Takes time | Trainees/apprentices |
| Hairdressing colleges | Trained. Low cost | Training standards vary | Junior stylists and trainees |
| Job centre | Low cost. Quick response | Quality unpredictable unless good rapport with JC | Any (best juniors) |
| Local papers | Quick response. Usually effective | Expensive. Quality often poor | Any |
| National press | Large response. Very effective/fast response. Non-locals | Very expensive. Requires professional copy | Any High fliers for top jobs |
| Local radio/TV | As national press plus attract locals | Very expensive. Needs recording | Any (top jobs best) |
| Specialist journals | Select audience. Good response usually | Slow. Copy deadlines. Expensive | Any (especially technical jobs) |
| Show window adverts | Cheap, quick. Attract locals | Must be tastefully done | Any (especially juniors) |
| Employment agencies | Selection done for you. Quality staff found. Reduce interviews | Expensive. Slow. May not know your market | Any (best better jobs) |
| Promotion | Cheap/quick. You know staff. Improves staff morale | You still need to recruit | Junior – full asst. man – manager etc. |

- Brief *description* of the *job*, its position in the organisation and relationships with other jobs
- Brief *description* of the *business* (where relevant)
- The ways in which the job makes any special demands or differs from a normal person's expectations, e.g. hours, travel, prospects, responsibility, safety, etc.
- The *minimum* requirements in terms of the seven-point plan demanded. Physical requirements are as important as qualifications/age/experience etc. *Be careful of Sex/Race Discrimination provisions.*
- Instructions as to how a candidate, if interested, should proceed further. A number of options are available:

  telephone
  send in a letter or complete an application form
  visit for discussion

In general use simple language and sentence structure ('*Daily Mirror* language') and aim to give candidates enough information to decide if they are interested and if they are suitable.

An additional objective of advertising is to build up a public image of the business through the advertising effort over a long period. It is this type of argument that often makes the use of house style/logo/agency particularly attractive.

*Seven-point checklist for advertisements*

(1) *Headline*
    The immediate identification of your potential candidate by a meaningful job title or the work subject.
(2) *Refining features*
    One or two words, or a short phrase, to amplify the above or unique interest factors which may cover industry, location or incentive.
(3) *The business*
    This should provide a brief understanding of your business to help build up interest and promote your advertisement against a competitor's who may have an identical post.

    - What it does
    - Size
    - Achievements
    - Growth in future
    - Future projects or development
    - Interest factors
    - Special features

(4) *The job*
    Brief details clarifying job, main duties and special features.

    - Reason for appointment
    - To whom responsible
    - Duties/tasks
    - Opportunities for personal development
    - Support (management and/or subordinates)
    - Interest factors

JUNIOR STYLISTS & STYLISTS                       CONFIDENTIAL

## APPLICATION FOR EMPLOYMENT

SURNAME AND
MAIDEN NAME IF APPLICABLE:                  OTHER NAMES:

HOME ADDRESS:                       Next of Kin:

Telephone No.:                      Address:

| Date of Birth | Place of Birth | Nationality | Married/Single | Children |
|---|---|---|---|---|
|  |  |  |  |  |

POSITION APPLIED FOR:

SOURCE OF APPLICATION: Newspaper/Agency/Friend please state:

DETAILS OF EDUCATION FROM AGE 11, include University Course and Part-time study

| Date started | Date left | Name & address of Schools, Colleges, University | Exams taken, subjects passed | Quals. & Grades |
|---|---|---|---|---|
|  |  |  |  |  |

Other training such as Evening classes:

APPRENTICESHIP:

| Date started | Date left | Name of Company | Salary | Reason for leaving |
|---|---|---|---|---|
|  |  |  |  |  |

LANGUAGES:                      Bilingual/Fluent/Useable

HOBBIES & INTERESTS (names of Societies/Institutions of which you are a member

MEDICAL HISTORY
Have you ever had or do you suffer from:-

Any serious illness . . . . . . . . . . . . . . . . . . . . . . . . . . . . . . . . . . . . Major operation . . . . . . . . . . . . . . . . . . . . . . . . . . . . . . . . . . .

Epileptic fits . . . . . . . . . . . . . . . . . . . . . . . . . . . . . . . . . . . . . . . . Asthma . . . . . . . . . . . . . . . . . . . . . . . . . . . . . . . . . . . . . . . . . . .

Bronchial disorders . . . . . . . . . . . . . . . . . . . . . . . . . . . . . . . . . . . Skin complaint . . . . . . . . . . . . . . . . . . . . . . . . . . . . . . . . . . . .

Are you willing to have a medical examination?     . . . . . . . . . . . . . . . . . . . . . . . . . . . . . . . . . . . . . . . . . . . . . . . . . . . . .

(5) *The requirements*
Candidate requirements summarised, but when possible, emphasising absolute essentials as opposed to preferences.

- Age
- Education and training
- Qualifications

**JOB HISTORY**  (start with most recent Company)

| Employer's name and address | From | To | Position held | Salary | Reason for leaving |
|---|---|---|---|---|---|
|  |  |  |  |  |  |

Notice of termination required by present employer? . . . . . . . . . . . . . . . . . . . . . . . . . . . . . . . . . . . . . . . . . . . . . .

When could you start? . . . . . . . . . . . . . . . . . . . . . . . . . . . .      Do you have any holidays already arranged?
. . . . . . . . . . . . . . . . . . . . . . . . . . . . . . . . . . . . . . . . . . . . . .

Have you ever been asked to resign or been dismissed? . . . . . . . . . . . . . . . . . . . . . . . . . . . . . . . . . . . . . . . . . . . . . . .

Give a brief reason why you wish to work for our Company? . . . . . . . . . . . . . . . . . . . . . . . . . . . . . . . . . . . . . . . . . . .
. . . . . . . . . . . . . . . . . . . . . . . . . . . . . . . . . . . . . . . . . . . . . . . . . . . . . . . . . . . . . . . . . . . . . . . . . . . . . . . . . . . . . .
. . . . . . . . . . . . . . . . . . . . . . . . . . . . . . . . . . . . . . . . . . . . . . . . . . . . . . . . . . . . . . . . . . . . . . . . . . . . . . . . . . . . . .

The Company may approach any of the Employers listed to provide a reference on your behalf.

Names and address of TWO people, not relatives, from whom personal references may be obtained:—

1.                                                                      2.

DECLARATION:

The above particulars are correct and I understand that all appointments are subject to:—

        a)     satisfactory references

        b)     the entries on this form being accurate, and

        c)     may be subject to a medical report

Signed . . . . . . . . . . . . . . . . . . . . . . . . . . . . . . . . . . . . .      Date . . . . . . . . . . . . . . . . . . . . . . . . . . . . . . . . . . . . .

**FOR OFFICE USE ONLY**

Starting date . . . . . . . . . . . . . . . . . . . . . . . . . . . . . . . .      Position . . . . . . . . . . . . . . . . . . . . . . . . . . . . . . . . . .

Salary . . . . . . . . . . . . . . . . . . . . . . . . . . . . . . . . . . . . . .      Full-time / part-time

Salon / Branch . . . . . . . . . . . . . . . . . . . . . . . . . . . . . .

References applied for:                                                 Received:

Interview Notes:

        10/80

**Fig. 3.10** Sample application for employment form.

- ● Experience (necessary years and particular methods worked or understood)
- ● Management techniques (if required)
- ● Specialities

(6) *Incentives*
- ● Pay

- Benefits, inducements, (commission, bonus, car, pension, holidays, removal assistance)
- Job satisfaction/interest
- Working conditions/equipment
- Prospects/development
- Location and travel prospects

(7) *Action*

This should be created with the candidate's habits in mind unless anonymity is required. Tell the candidate what to do.

- Telephone
- Call in/visit
- Write in for information/application form

## 3.7 Initial selection

If you have carried out all the previous stages correctly in a real situation you will have drafted an advert and may have placed your advert. So people are either ringing up, or writing, or calling in. Now you need to begin collecting your information in a systematic way and for that we use an application form.

The application form serves as a quick and easy way of collecting much of the information we need about our possible new staff member. Experience has shown that very few people in the hairdressing industry have used application forms yet this is one of the quickest forms of:

- Collecting information
- Screening out those people unsuitable for the job

Figure 3.10 shows an application form specially designed for the hairdressing industry. All applicants should complete this as it forms the first key part in the selection process. Application forms of this kind are useful for a number of reasons:

(1) It collects the same information on every applicant.
(2) It is a valuable aid to the interviewer. It gives basic information and highlights areas to question.
(3) If the person is selected it can form the basis of his/her personnel (and personal) record.
(4) It will tell you the kind of people who saw your advert and who want to come and work for you.

Remember, too, to be observant if the applicant comes into the salon or rings up or even writes a letter in to you:

- What did they look like?
- How did they speak? Confidently? Brightly?
- What was their handwriting/spelling/English like?

You must adopt the detective role always looking for new clues.

Many salons, when candidates apply, send not only an application form but also further information/details on the job, salon etc. This can be useful as it saves explanation in the interview and allows the time to be more profitably used.

Now let us assume you have a number of returned completed application forms. Now you can use your 'seven-point plan' person specification to sift through the candidates and to identify which one(s) you wish to interview. Sort them into three piles – *possibles*, *doubtfuls* and *rejects* – according to whether they meet the criteria you have used, e.g. suppose you had three applicants – the data might be:

|  | | Copied from forms | | |
|---|---|---|---|---|
| Item | Required | Person A | Person B | Person C |
| Age | 21–30 | 35 | 24 | 21 |
| Experience | 2–3 years | 7 | 3 | 2 |
| Health | excellent | poor | very good | ? |

This would make A a reject, B a possible and C a doubtful. Would you agree?

Now interview only the possibles unless there are only one or two, in which case look very carefully at the doubtfuls to see if they might be worth a chance. Notice how this analysis will help you interview by identifying areas of uncertainty, e.g. you would ask C about their health.

So now you have decided which of the potential candidates to interview you need to write or telephone and invite them. Include details of how to get to you and be sure they are clear as to time and place and tell them how long it will take. If you need other staff to be present then make sure they will be there. Let candidates know if you are not going to interview them and thank them for applying. Be polite and don't hurt feelings.

So we come to the day of the interview. Make sure you read each applicant's form before you interview them, and identify the areas which you particularly wish to question them on. Make sure you have all your papers with you:

- Job description
- Person specification
- Application form
- Notes/questions

Make the necessary arrangements to see their work if this is going to be necessary. You may like to prepare *questions in advance*. Many professional interviewers do this.

The five basic rules of interviewing are:

(1) Preparation before interview.
(2) Establish rapport with the candidates.
(3) Structure the content of the interview in order to get the information *you* want.
(4) Control the interview in an unobtrusive way so that it appears logical.
(5) Give the candidates the information *they* want to make a decision.

We discuss interviewing skills and techniques in more detail in the next section.

## 3.8 The interview

What is the secret of good interviewing? Many books have been written on this subject but we indicate the guidelines we feel you need to bear in mind when interviewing. The key points are to:

(1) establish rapport and ensure that the candidate will talk freely with you
(2) structure content to obtain the information that you require
(3) control structure to keep on track and collect relevant information

### 3.8.1 Opening the interview

(1) It is vital here to establish rapport. Introduce yourself. Welcome the candidate. Offer coffee/tea etc. Make a small amount of small talk, e.g. how did they get here, what do they think of the salon?
(2) Next explain to the candidate exactly what will happen to him/her, i.e. practical test and when he/she will know if they are successful.
(3) Beware of immediate impressions. They are usually false.
(4) Mention you intend to take notes if you intend to.

### 3.8.2 Running the interview

(1) The aims are to get the person to talk freely and openly about relevant areas and to check out specific information.
(2) Remember you also need to complete the information on all the candidates as per your person specification.
(3) One of the common sequences used in interviews is:

- What they are doing now – skills etc.
- What they have done in the past – skills etc.
- What they want for the future – development/ambition
- Why they have applied for the job
- What about leisure activities/interests
- Their family background and personal circumstances
- Check facts collected
- Allow candidate to ask questions or to offer any additional items about him/herself
- Close interview – see later

The first two items are relative 'safe' areas and candidates can relax and discuss themselves freely before you move onto more searching areas.

We discuss questions and questioning techniques in the following section.

*Questions and questioning techniques*

Interviewers distinguish between a number of types of questions – namely:

- Open
- Closed
- Probing
- Multiple
- Leading
- Ambiguous
- Linking

Some of these are to be avoided, but others have different levels of usefulness. We discuss the main types below.

*Open questions* are particularly useful in that the candidate has to give information and by acting on this the interviewer can follow on and investigate points.
e.g. 'What do you enjoy doing in your spare time?' or 'Tell me about your present job?'

*Closed questions* are questions with yes/no answers and are useful for

checking points but bad interviewers use too many and they make the interviewer do all the work.
e.g. 'You left XYZ in April?' (Answer: Yes or No)

*Probing questions* follow on and investigate areas of interest in more depth. They get to the real issues.
e.g. 'Tell me why you left . . .'.
A useful trick is to remember the sequence:

● Open
● Close
● Probe

e.g.
'Tell me about your last job.'      (open)
'It was awful, well pretty bad.'
'So you didn't like it much.'      (closed)
'No.'
'Why exactly was that?'      (probe)

This is a powerful technique.

*Multiple questions* are to be avoided and are where the interviewer asks more than one question at the same time.

**Fig. 3.11** Sample interviewing questions.

'Tell me about ..............................'

'Please go on ..............................'

'That is interesting. Tell me more ..............................'

'What exactly do you mean by ..............................'

'What do you like best about ..............................'

'What do you like least about ..............................'

'What did you enjoy most ..............................'

'How did you feel about ..............................'

'Why did you ..............................'

'What did you ..............................'

'Who did you ..............................'

'Where did you ..............................'

'When did you ..............................'

'What exactly happened ..............................'

e.g. 'Did you want to go into hairdressing or did you prefer beauty therapy, or perhaps you wanted to stay on at school, or was it your preference to get married?'

*Leading questions* are also to be avoided and are questions which contain the answer, i.e. the interviewee knows what you want?
e.g. 'You wouldn't want to move in the next year . . .?'
'Is your health good?'
You will tend to get the answer you want rather than the truth with leading questions.

*Ambiguous questions* are also to be avoided as are unclear questions, i.e. where people can misunderstand the question.
e.g. 'Do you chat to clients?' could mean:

● Do you talk to them, i.e. friendly
● Do you talk to them all the time, i.e. 'chatter on'

So when the person answers – which do they mean? Using simple, clear and precise language bearing in mind the needs of your interviewee is the secret.

*Linking questions* are useful whenever you wish to move onto a new topic or develop logic – they are often reflective.
e.g. 'So you left school . . . then . . . so what do you wish to do next?' They link the various sections of the interview together.

Some interviewers learn questions and we have recorded some generally useful ones in Fig. 3.11. You might like to look at these and categorise them to help you at the interviewing stage.

### 3.8.3 Ending the interview

(1) The candidate may well decide he or she isn't interested in which case thank them and close the interview.
(2) If you are unhappy with the candidate thank them for coming and say you will get in touch (indicate *when*).
(3) If you think the candidate is a strong one then check vital details, e.g. availability/salary etc. You may want to arrange a second interview.

In any case make sure you thank them for coming and *do* contact them. Courtesy costs little and does a lot for your reputation.

### 3.8.4 Immediately after the interview

(1) Write up your notes immediately and check your findings against the specification.
(2) Draw a conclusion about whether the candidate is *strong*, *medium* or *weak* in terms of what you wish and note particularly the *good* and *bad* features.
(3) Review your own interviewing technique. Was it fair? Did I get all the information I needed?

*Self review is the key to interview success!*
You may have the interview within a framework which involves the use of other kinds of tests/measures, e.g.:

● Written tests

- Trade tests/practicals
- References, etc

In the next section we show you other methods and look at their usefulness as a means of improving selection.

### 3.8.5 *Basic interviewing checklist*

(1) Decide in advance the purpose of the interview and the key areas you wish to examine in it.
(2) Collect in advance as many relevant facts as possible (e.g. a job specification and completed application form and the person specification).
(3) Think in advance about the interview:

- Study the information available against the criteria you have set.
- Consider the context of the interview and the known characteristics and expectations of the interviewee and decide what behaviour would be most appropriate.
- Decide on the main points you need to cover in terms of *both giving* and *obtaining* information.
- Consider the type of question which will encourage unbiased response.
- Plan a (flexible) scheme.
- Decide on roles for each member of the panel (if appropriate).

(4) Inform the person to be interviewed in a way which does not arouse anxiety or hostility (e.g. by an informal letter; by keeping to appointment times so that he or she does not wait and wonder).
(5) Open the interview in a way which puts the interviewee at ease. Avoid rushing to the most significant or complex topic before the person is fully at ease.
(6) Interview in comfortable surroundings. Consider the impact that the location and its layout will have upon the interviewee. The aim is to make the candidate feel at ease.
(7) Avoid interruptions, e.g. try to have telephone calls transferred. Try to put other pressing matters out of your mind.
(8) Interview alone wherever possible. When you must interview with another interviewer, give careful consideration to your respective roles and the effects of your interactions on the interviewee.
(9) Preserve an atmosphere of calm. Never show that you have other things to do. Do not argue with the interviewee.
(10) Talk as little as you possibly can. Aim for the candidate to give you as much as possible.
(11) Do not interrupt; do not criticise; do not make moral judgements about opinions expressed (even favourable ones); do not express your own opinions (even by leading questions).
(12) Listen to what the interviewee says; listen for things that are not or cannot be said; and show that you are listening. Be interested in the candidate and what he/she has to say.
(13) Look for underlying feelings and attitudes.
(14) Summarise from time to time. It helps the person being interviewed to realise your interest and to see problems more clearly. It also checks out that you have understood the replies.
(15) Ask questions

- Which need more than yes or no for an answer
- Which do not suggest how they should be answered
- Which require specific replies
- Which help to reveal feelings
- Which are unambiguous
- Which are clear and comprehensible

(16)  Time your questions. Follow the interviewee's lead whenever possible. Keep difficult questions until confidence is established. Keep the interview relevant. Be sensitive to the interviewee.

(17)  Recognise your own biases/prejudices/stereotypes

- Personal prejudices and associations, e.g. He looks like the last person (awful!). Crooked stockings mean an untidy mind. A dead fish handshake means a flabby personality.
- Too much reliance on outstanding merits and demerits (halo effect).

(18)  Do not try to achieve too much in one interview. Set a realistic finishing time and handle what cannot be achieved by that time on another occasion.

(19)  Agree on future action with the interviewee and inform the interviewee of what is to happen.

(20)  Leave the person being interviewed with the feeling that he or she has had a satisfactory hearing. Give an opportunity to ask questions and give reasonable answers if you can.

*After the interview*

- Aim for a balanced judgement.
- Take notes while impressions are still fresh (to counteract halo effect).
- Collect collaborative evidence, references, test results, etc. where appropriate.
- Take any necessary action promptly.
- Compare candidates against the criteria developed in the employee specification.
- Decide whether you have a poor/average/good candidate and note specific strengths and weaknesses.
- Question yourself: 'Did I give a fair interview?'

## 3.9  Other methods of selection

The evidence on interviews is that they are not particularly valid as a means of selection and it is a common observation that mistakes can in fact occur. This is no justification for poor interviewing however as this will simply worsen the situation further. Perhaps an analogy would be to try to cut grass with scissors – not particularly suitable but sharp scissors would certainly be better than blunt ones.

However, remembering that the aim of the selection interview is to gain information then there are other ways we can obtain information about candidates. Figure 3.12 shows areas of interest and the selection techniques available to us. Notice that the interview is the best single way and all the other methods supplement and check it.

These alternative methods can support the interview however and the

**Fig. 3.12**
Sources of
information about
candidates.

| Area of interest | Method(s) available |
|---|---|
| (1) Physical appearance, health etc. | Interview/observation<br>Medical examination<br>References |
| (2) Attainments or achievements | School records/certificates<br>Work experience/references<br>Interview<br>Trade tests<br>Demonstration/practical |
| (3) Intelligence | Interview<br>Tests |
| (4) Special capabilities or aptitudes, e.g. numeracy | Interview<br>Tests |
| (5) Personal interests or leisure activities | Interview<br>Checklists<br>Tests |
| (6) Disposition or personality factors | Interview/references<br>School records/personality tests |
| (7) Personal circumstances | Interview |
| (8) Motivation to work | Interview/references<br>Tests |

evidence is that they will make it more realistic and hence more valid. The problem is that in some cases these alternatives may be unreliable and we have to cross-check the information. Also some of these techniques require expert use and interpretation and are not for the amateur interviewer. The methods discussed below are:

(1) References
(2) Medical examination
(3) Use of school reports/records/certificates
(4) Demonstration/practicals
(5) Tests and checklists
(6) Use of outside consultants or selection agencies
(7) Probation period

### 3.9.1 References

References should be used to check *factual data only* in most cases, e.g.:

• Date of joining
• Date of leaving
• Job/duties
• Salary
• Days absent etc.

Under these questions most people will give honest and truthful answers.
   If you know the *referee* personally then it may be worth asking for other

information if you know that person to be genuinely honest and truthful. Otherwise the information may be suspect. The telephone is the quickest method to obtain such references. Ask the candidate for permission to do so *beforehand* though.

### 3.9.2 Medical examinations

These are essential for senior positions especially if you have extensive pension or sick pay schemes.

Many hairdressers ask *all* new staff for a doctor's report (at employer's expense) as a means of checking they are not ill, do not have infectious diseases etc. (Doctors will only send this information to you if the candidate permits.)

Our view would be to obtain a doctor's report for people in senior positions who have extensive pension or sick pay schemes or if you have any concern that the candidate's health may be suspect.

### 3.9.3 Use of school reports/records/certificates

School certificates etc. are useful evidence that qualifications have been obtained and that training has been undergone. It is not uncommon for candidates to pretend to have done things they have not.

School reports are often illuminating insights into the candidates personality and for young school-leavers possibly the only evidence of what they are actually like. Use these carefully however and take the overall view – sometimes teachers don't get on with students and so on. Use them as a check against your own findings.

### 3.9.4 Use of demonstrations/practicals

This is clearly a most powerful method of finding out what candidates can do. Note that although many hairdressers use it to see how technically competent candidates are, you could also use it to see how candidates deal with clients and their selling skills – two difficult areas to measure. You could do this by *role play* i.e. get one of the staff to 'play' a customer and the candidate to 'play' the stylist and look at how they perform.

These methods could also be used to look at the manner in which receptionists answer the phone or managers talk to staff etc. In the US many interviewers use long periods of such methods to try to see how people will actually perform 'on the job' before taking them on to do that job.

### 3.9.5 Use of tests

There are probably no selection methods more misunderstood, misinterpreted or abused than tests. For our purposes we consider tests of four types:

(1) 'Trade tests'
(2) Simple skills tests
(3) Aptitude tests
(4) Personality tests/interest inventories

In all cases the user of the test *must be properly trained to administer it and use it*. This means in the case of (4) a psychologist or trained tester. Also only use tests which have been properly designed, tested and validated for the purpose for which you intend to use them. Improperly used tests are:

- Immoral and possibly illegal
- A waste of time as they give no useful information
- Cause loss of faith in test procedures.

We have been appalled at the abuses we have seen and by no means only in the hairdressing industry.

*Trade tests* are special tests designed to test knowledge of facts/skills needed to do the job. They have been designed specially for the trade and are a measure of how much the person knows about the job. Sometimes they are written (pen/pencil), sometimes they are practical, sometimes a mixture of the two. They are useful for testing areas of professional competence.

e.g. How many towels should you use for shampooing? . . . Why?

ISM can provide specially designed tests of this type if required.

*Simple skills tests* test additional abilities and skills and might for example:

- Ask candidate to 'cash up'
- Ask candidate to add up figures and calculate wages
- Test client handling or selling skills

These are useful as a way of checking the impression at interview against factual data.

*Aptitude tests* test not a skill but ability and hence potential for achieving certain skills, e.g.:

- Numerical aptitudes (numbers)
- Verbal aptitude (words)
- Reasoning and intelligence and so on

These are useful for young people who have not yet had the opportunity to acquire skills. You need to know if they have the potential to do so.

*Personality tests/inventories* try to assess a person's personality, or creativity or attitudes or interests (depending on the exact test). These are among the most controversial tests and are usually best used (if required) by trained people (psychologists or teachers) but they can be used to check one's own impression from the interview. Interest inventories particularly look at your hobbies/interests and some interesting work in the US/UK has indicated that successful people in certain kinds of jobs seem to have similar hobbies/interests (and these are different from other groups and jobs). No conclusive data exists for hairdressing but it is an interesting area. ISM would be pleased to advise you on any aspects of testing as part of their usual consultancy activity.

### 3.9.6 Use of outside consultants/agencies

*Consultants* can help in a number of areas:

- Improving your selection procedure and documentation
- Interviewing skills training for you and your staff
- Selecting appropriate tests
- Interviewing senior staff with you

They are not cheap but you will get a good level of service, expertise and value for money if you are careful.

*Employment agencies* will for a fee help you to recruit staff. This can be particularly useful for special staff, e.g. receptionists and managers.

### 3.9.7 Probation period

We say more about this in Section 3.11 Integration of new staff, but you should remember that this is in one sense part of your selection process as it is an ideal time to correct any errors that may occur during the initial employment period.

## 3.10 Terms and conditions of employment

Now you have decided the person you wish to employ you should do a number of other things:

(1) Check he/she wants to come and when etc.
(2) Write to all unsuccessful candidates.
(3) Send new recruit contract of employment and joining information.
(4) Inform other staff of new person's arrival.
(5) Make arrangements for induction.

A Contract of Employment or written particulars of an employee's terms and conditions of employment is important for all employees and Fig. 3.13 shows what should go into a Contract of Employment. This shows the new recruit all the relevant parts of his/her employment relationship and helps him/her to understand exactly what is involved.

**Fig. 3.13** What should go into a Contract of Employment.

- Names and addresses of parties
- Date of commencement
- Scale or rate of pay or method of calculation of pay
- How/When paid
- Hours of work
- Holiday entitlements
- Sickness absence arrangements and sick pay scheme details
- Pension scheme details
- Maternity leave provision
- Job title
- Notice period required by both sides before termination
- Disciplinary procedure (including rules)
- Grievance procedure
- Union membership details
- Health and safety provision
- Details of any probation period

These are not always spelt out in detail but one can refer to other documents, e.g. job description/rules etc. These must be available (e.g. on a noticeboard or in a staff manual) for scrutiny.

*Radius clauses*

Many salons often ask about radius clauses and it is perfectly possible to incorporate one of these into a Contract of Employment. The key things to remember about radius clauses are:

- They act as a deterrent but can be difficult to enforce unless they are reasonable
- They must have a distance element
- They must have a time element, e.g. one mile restriction for six months

If the salon trades in a busy town then it is much more likely that a radius restriction clause of half a mile and six months would be reasonable and in a city a quarter of a mile for three months.

## 3.11 Integration of new staff

Informing staff of the new appointment is important if they are to welcome them and give them the initial help and support required during their introductory period. Many salons do not concentrate enough time and thought into this aspect of their business and it is for this reason that staff take longer to integrate into their new environment. In fact, research shows that many people leave salons within the first three months of their employment due to lack of thought in this area. In the next section we concentrate on induction training and training requirements.

*Induction*

Some (larger) salons have a formal induction period to familiarise staff with everything. Others produce a Company Handbook but whatever it is called it needs to tell the new recruit about the items covered by the contract as shown in Fig. 3.13. In addition, the following areas should be included:

- A brief description of the company and its history
- Promotion and training opportunities
- Medical and first aid facilities
- Restaurant/canteen arrangements
- Social/welfare arrangements
- Telephone calls and letters
- Travelling/subsistence

This may be a booklet or just a typed document.
The induction process is designed to:

- familiarise new employees and put them at ease
- interest them (motivate) in the new job
- provide basic information about the new job/company
- indicate standards and behaviour expected from them
- show them prospects of development in the company
- provide product knowledge training, e.g. if a stylist is familiar with one major manufacturer's products and your salon uses another product range then it is essential that product knowledge training is given at this stage if the salon wishes to ensure productivity is reached within a short space of time

- provide training in the new skills that the new employee does not possess, starting as soon as possible after employment

The aim is to encourage and to motivate staff to stay. Remember perfect jobs for perfect people do not exist! We must, when employing staff, identify the gaps in their skills and ensure that the new skills or re-training skills required are introduced at this stage. It is lack of training, not just in procedures but in skill knowledge, that is one of the greatest reasons why staff do not integrate quickly into a new environment.

*Trial period*

A trial period can be used to see if both sides are suited. Although this can be useful, salon owners should beware of using it as a substitute for good selection as you should only not renew contracts for extreme reasons, usually discipline/behaviour, and not incompetence. 'Hire and fire' policies demotivate *all* staff and should be avoided if at all possible.

You have now learnt the whole process of:

- Analysing the job
- Deciding the person you are looking for
- Recruiting them
- Selecting them
- Taking them on and inducting them

If you implement what we have suggested then you have the key to successful salons – good staff!

Good staff, as many salon owners are aware, do not just happen, they are created by the amount of time, energy and training that is invested in them. In our opinion, training is the answer to all of the ills of the hairdressing industry and those salons that have recognised this element and use it effectively are the ones that will have successful salons.

### 3.11.1 Induction training

In the previous section, we stressed how important it was to integrate new staff so they became effective in the shortest possible time. The hairdressing industry lacks a minimum standard of skills required to be able to do the job of hairdresser, hairdressing manager or salon owner so that when we recruit new staff they bring with them methods and ways of working which we may not like. It is the salon owner or manager's responsibility to ensure that staff are able to work within their framework unless they want to adopt the new employee's methods of work.

We have already mentioned that there will never be perfect peole for perfect jobs – we must make square pegs fit into round holes by *training*.

Training can be categorised into the following areas:

- Trainee/apprenticeship training
- Technical training, e.g. perming and colouring, hairdressing
- Communication skills training
- Service skills training
- Administrative/systems training
- Management training

*Trainees/apprentices*

Traditionally, the industry has trained apprentices and trainees by the 'sitting watching Nelly' or 'watch what I do then have a go yourself' approach. Some salons train staff by the watching and practising approach but use colleges or manufacturers to help them with the technical and theoretical side of hairdressing.

Most salons, however, train staff in the evenings on the pretext that working on models affects the service to clients. But why do we employ trainees anyway? Are they cleaners and coffee makers or do we wish to develop staff at the optimum pace in order to employ them as stylists in the shortest possible time? If we want cleaners and coffee makers why don't we employ assistants to do these menial tasks?

Anyone who has ever gone to adult evening classes or had to study a new subject will tell you how tired they are at the end of the day. Our ability to absorb new information when we are tired is limited, which is why it takes so long to learn! Add to the tiredness factor the fact that most trainees are also trying to acclimatise themselves to working long hours and standing all day after many years of school hours and it is not surprising that an apprentice, on this basis, takes two to three years to learn hairdressing skills. In fact, most trainees receive three hours training per week, 44 weeks a year (deducting seasonally busy times and holidays) which means they receive 49 days of training or 396 hours to become a hairdresser!

If we trained trainees one full day a week we would complete their training in 12 to 18 months and still during that time give them ample opportunity to practise.

*Decline of school leavers*

Due to the drop in school leavers available for employment, the industry is now competing for the same people as other sectors of industry. This has been caused by:

- Reduction in the birth rate during the 1970s which continued until 1984
- Parents encouraging children to obtain qualifications and higher education
- Parents/children wanting high pay upon leaving school

Banks, insurance companies, the armed forces, the police force, hotels, catering and retailing are all competing for school leavers. The question we must ask within the hairdressing industry is why should young people want to work in hairdressing? What does it have to offer?

At the moment it has the image of offering:

- Low pay
- Poor quality training
- Bad conditions of employment
- Fragmented career opportunities

We must make the industry more attractive in the future by the following approach:

- Formalised, systematic training held during the day in the company's time
- Recognised qualifications
- Shorter training period, e.g. 12–18 months

- Realistic pay
- Terms and conditions of employment comparable to other industries, e.g. holidays, sick pay
- Promote career opportunities
- Offer on-going training

*Technical training*

The most profitable area of a hairdressing business is the technical services we offer clients – if we get our prices right, train staff to work at speed and to sell the services with confidence.

Many staff do not sell technical services because they do not feel confident about this side of their work. There are salons who train their staff in perming and colouring techniques, ensuring they understand the theory and have product knowledge and continue to receive on-going creative training in technical work. *The majority, however, do not.*

That is why salons are frequently looking for staff knowledgeable in colouring and perming and is one of the reasons why manufacturers offer courses on technical work to ensure stylists become competent and confident at technical work.

We must ensure staff are thoroughly trained in this area otherwise they will not sell technical services. Promoting these services becomes a waste of money if the staff lack confidence to carry out the work. In fact, colouring is one of the most profitable areas of hairdressing yet, along with retailing, is the greatest weakness within the industry. Recent manufacturers' surveys show that the entire industry generates just 7 per cent of hairdressing services from colouring. A sad state of affairs. No wonder the chemists and supermarkets are laughing all the way to the bank!

*Communications skills training*

If staff were asked to write down how much of their day is spent communicating they would find that 80 per cent of their time is occupied in giving information and listening. Analyse the job of a stylist and we find that 40 per cent of the work of the hairdresser is practical skills such as hairdressing, paperwork and cleaning and 60 per cent communication skills.

To be able to communicate is not a talent – it is a *skill*. We can all learn to communicate effectively if we want to and, more importantly, if we realise how important it is so that our working day runs smoothly. Yet many stylists have spent a number of years learning how to cut, colour and perm hair but have never been trained in how to talk and listen to clients. We have all heard of brilliant hairdressers who are creative and produce fabulous haircuts but they do not talk to their clients. The client begins to think that she has upset the stylist.

If we look at the cycle of communication in a salon, we will see that from when a client first contacts us to when she leaves communication is vital. We must communicate effectively at the consultation stage because it is *this stage where misunderstandings begin*. The client is trying to express what she wants, the stylist fails to understand what she requires, so she leaves the salon unhappy or dissatisfied with the service or style she has received.

At the backwash, we can begin to reinforce what was said at the consultation stage or to sow the seed of the products which we will be using on her hair. How many times have you heard at the backwash a trainee asking a client 'do you want a conditioner' or 'I don't really use the products myself'?

When the client reaches the styling position, how many times does the stylist listen *actively* to what the client is saying or recognise the signals which indicate an interest in additional services? We are often too busy being concerned about what else is going on in the salon to notice.

When the client goes to the reception area to pay her bill how often do we check that she is happy with her hair and the service she has received? The correct questioning techniques at this stage will help us to identify how she feels. It is also the key time to ensure she rebooks for a future appointment.

Finally, how often do we place emphasis upon the client departing and thanking her for her custom so that she leaves with a good impression?

Communication skills training must cover how to give and receive information and the part our body language plays in communicating. We must learn that it is not what we say but the way that we say it that generatives a positive response. We need to learn questioning techniques to extract information from clients and to learn to actively listen. We need to be aware of the physical and emotional barriers that prevent us from listening so that we can overcome them. All of these skills are crucial if we wish to be successful hairdressers.

*Service skills training*

We have already mentioned that the industry places too little emphasis upon communication skills but another area of neglect is that of service training. Many hairdressers believe that their job is to produce high quality work whereas in fact it is just as important if not more so to make the client happy to part with her money.

Market research shows that clients visit a particular salon for a variety of reasons (see Fig. 1.1). Very few of them are to do with hairdressing. It is service, personality and atmosphere which make clients return regularly.

How much training is given within the salon on offering *a consistent standard of service* because the salon has not clearly identified how each client should be treated? Look at the following areas and tick which ones are clearly defined within the salon:

|  | Clear procedure | No procedure |
|---|---|---|
| (1) Telephone technique | ———— | ———— |
| (2) Welcome procedure | ———— | ———— |
| (3) Collecting client information | ———— | ———— |
| (4) Coat/gowning-up procedure on arrival | ———— | ———— |
| (5) Consultation | ———— | ———— |
| (6) Home care advice | ———— | ———— |
| (7) Backwash procedure | ———— | ———— |
| (8) Refreshments | ———— | ———— |
| (9) Styling position procedure | ———— | ———— |

| | Clear procedure | No procedure |
|---|---|---|
| (10) Home care advice by stylist | _____ | _____ |
| (11) Check-out procedure – settling the bill | _____ | _____ |
| (12) Coat/gowning procedure on departure | _____ | _____ |
| (13) Booking appointments | _____ | _____ |
| (14) Hair care advice | _____ | _____ |

If you are a salon owner or manager reading this book ask your staff what they think is the procedure in each area. The answers may surprise you.

Market research also shows that clients want more information on home care advice yet we seem reticent at providing it. Why is this? Professional advice on hair care products from supermarkets and chemists does not happen so we must use our knowledge to ensure the client feels confident of our services – *otherwise why should the client visit our salon instead of our competitor?*

*Administrative/systems training*

Hairdressers often hate paperwork and systems of any kind but without them salons cannot function. The more a salon group expands, the more systems and procedures are required. Without them the salon is chaos and projects a disorganised image to the client as well as making it more stressful for the staff to function on a daily basis.

Training must be given in salons to ensure the systems are understood and continue to function. The following areas need systems to make the salon function smoothly:

- Appointment system
- Bill procedure
- Client record cards
- Technical records
- Cashing-up procedure
- Recording client service information
- Holiday records
- Absentee procedure
- Time keeping
- Stock control

*Management training*

Many staff promoted into management or supervisory positions do not receive any kind of management training. Out of 165 000 people employed in hairdressing, only 2000 have ever been on any kind of management training course or seminar. The UK invests less money in training, particularly management training, than any other country in Europe. If we wish to overcome the skills shortage at management level first and foremost we must train people, by developing our staff to set standards of professionalism within the industry.

At present, the process of developing management tends to be 'sink or swim'. Unfortunately, many people drown this way or lose their confidence so that they never want to try again. We must have recognised qualifications within the industry such as the City and Guilds/Hairdressing Training Board Certificate in Hairdressing Management 311. This would set a standard of the way we run our businesses in the future. In many European countries at the present time hairdressers are unable to open hairdressing salons unless they have passed a Master's Certificate or employ someone within their organisation who has passed this certificate.

Few managers are given job descriptions which clearly define their responsibilities and their levels of authority (see Section 3.3). For example how much authority does a manager have to recruit or terminate staff?

Many managers often feel their job is dealing with problems and aggravation from both sides – staff and salon owners – without any clearly defined areas of responsibility and authority. An impossible situation in which to function effectively, which is one of the reasons why managers become demotivated, opt out of making decisions or pass the buck up or down the hierarchy.

Having a clearly defined job description is no use whatsoever if the person responsible for doing the job does not *know how to do it*. Staff must be trained in the principles of managing and how to develop their skills to accept the responsibilities of the job. Without training a job description is a useless document.

Those salon managers or owners who have been managing for several years need to recognise that they continually need to be effective and ahead of their competitors. They must learn how to train the staff that they have and how to manage the most valuable asset in their business – people. Without the people, salon owners and managers might just as well rent a chair in a salon or become a home hairdresser. Staff who have a good education and receive training and development, however, will question and challenge decisions made by managers and salon owners. We can overcome this by involving staff in the way we run our businesses and by consulting them. We must reward the staff that work for our businesses, not just financially but by recognition, by praising them and, certainly at management level, by giving them a profit share of the business. It is better to give part of the profit back to the staff as opposed to spending years training and developing them only to find that because they are not rewarded accordingly or consulted they open up their own businesses in direct competition.

This approach may sound totally alien to some salon owners but we do not live in the days of the lord of the manor and the serfs and we cannot run our businesses in this way if we wish staff to continue to work for us and to be committed and motivated. We must involve them, share our successes with them and develop them wherever possible.

# Chapter Four
# Managing people

## 4.1 What is managing?

It is not our intention in this chapter to re-write all the management theories which can be obtained from the local library, but we have listed in the Appendix some recommended books for those readers who wish to pursue this subject in greater depth.

Ask a salon owner what is meant by 'managing' and the answer will be many different things. Ask a trainee the same question and the answer will be very different. For simplicity's sake, managing people falls into six main categories. The manager is:

- Leader
- Communicator
- Trainer
- Umpire
- Counsellor
- Worker

### 4.1.1 The manager as leader

To lead a team of people means to take responsibility not only for your own work but for other people's. There are advantages and disadvantages to this. It means taking the criticisms when the team fail but, conversely, receiving the praise (or part of it) when they get it right. This means often having to face both ways at the same time – to be loyal to the team and loyal to the salon owner and company. Not the easiest of tasks.

To be successful at leading we need to clearly define the goals and objectives in order that the team know what is expected of them and that they will have some measurement of when they have reached the goals. You may create a good or a bad team or, even worse, a mediocre one. A happy team usually produces good work. As a leader you are the centre of it – the work continues around you.

*Leading from the front*

We must all lead by example. In other words we cannot have one set of rules for the staff which, as the leader, we continually break. This will result in the manager losing credibility and eventually the staff's respect.

There are consequences of leading the team from the front, for example, by always using our own ideas, or worse, using the staff's ideas but not giving them credit for them. Managers that think for their staff and tell them what to do instead of involving them in the decision-making process will demotivate them and create lack of commitment and resentment. Most staff hate being told to do things but will happily carry out an instruction if you have explained why you want it done and the reasons behind it.

*Leading from behind or the centre*

Many staff, if presented with a problem, will often, with some guidelines, be able to come to a logical conclusion as to what action needs to be taken to overcome it. The job of manager is to keep the team focused on the problems so that, like driving a car, they stay on the road and get to their destination. It is much more fun if the team are involved in arriving at the destination instead of just being passengers. We can do this in the following two ways.

*Delegating fairly and sensibly*

Delegation means not just getting to those that are willing to do the work or jobs that we find unpleasant ourselves or to those we don't like. We must arrange the work so everyone contributes to the best of their ability.

*Focusing the team*

Concentrate on the problems not the people. We can never change personalities but we can solve problems. Explain the problem clearly and the guidelines under which they must make a decision, for example, a time factor, cost, manpower and expertise.

Once a decision has been made ensure it is followed through. If the decision cannot be put into action then explain why not.

*Be loyal upwards*

The manager represents the salon owner's or company's viewpoint. Passing the buck loses credibility, for example when we use excuses for unpopular decisions by saying 'the salon owner says . . .' or 'head office says we must . . .'. This is not managing – it is opting out of responsibility for the company decision. If you disagree with the policy decision then your views should be made known out of the hearing of the staff and through the appropriate channels. If there aren't any satisfactory channels find out why not.

*Be loyal downwards*

The staff must know that you represent their views fairly if they have a genuine complaint or reasonable criticism.

*Face the problems*

Managing means facing the problems as and when they occur. Putting off dealing with them does not make them go away. What may not appear to be important to you will certainly be important to the staff. Indecision on holidays, time off for special occasions or wage and commission queries all can be explosive if not dealt with quickly. Better to make a decision, even if it is difficult, provided you have acted fairly.

### 4.1.2 The manager as communicator

Anyone who leads a team needs to communicate with them. Communication is a two-way process – we must give information and keep the team informed but, just as importantly, we must make time to listen.

There are many barriers to listening which we need to be aware of (see Section 4.2 Communication for further information on this). The following action will help communication to be more effective.

*Make sure the team knows what they have to do and why*

This means explaining the goals and objectives of the team and the particular task that has been set. Explain why it is important and tell or show them how to achieve it.

*Listen to the team's views*

Have regular meetings even if you work with them on the salon floor every day. Set time aside for regular, if brief, meetings with your staff, not only to pass on information but to invite comments and listen to suggestions.

*Tell superiors what is happening and pass on the staff's views*

There is no point in consulting your staff unless you pass on the findings or any queries that they raise to higher management. This does not mean discussing all the detail with your boss but he or she should know what is going on and what people are thinking so that they are not faced suddenly with an unexpected crisis.

*Keep in touch with other managers and colleagues*

By keeping in touch with colleagues or managers and comparing notes with them you will be able to plan your own tasks more effectively. Managers who have been in the job longer may approach problems or situations differently from you. We can all learn from each other, even from newly appointed managers who may take a completely different approach. Many managers, particularly in larger salon groups, complain that they feel isolated and out of touch with what is going on in the rest of the organisation. This does not necessarily mean more frequent management meetings – all you have to do is pick up the telephone or have an informal chat with colleagues to find out what is going on.

### 4.1.3 *The manager as trainer*

As head of the team the staff will rely upon you to teach them the 'tricks of the trade'. You will already be skilled in many of their tasks. Part of the job is to pass on your knowledge in a way and at a speed that is suitable for them (see section 4.2 Communication and Chapter 6 Training).

There may be some tasks with which you are not familiar, either because you have never had to do them or because it is some time since you did them. It is impossible to be able to carry out *every* aspect of your staff's job as capably as them. Acknowledging that you can learn from them too will help them feel they have a genuine working partnership instead of a 'know-it-all, seen-it-all, done-it-all' manager. We must, therefore, ensure the following:

- Understand fully the job of each member of staff
- Ensure that each team member understands the job and can do the job
- Do not be afraid to learn even from subordinates

### 4.1.4 *The manager as umpire*

The manager as referee or umpire means being seen to be fair. This sometimes means not being the most popular person, but if you fail to enforce the company's regulations when someone breaks the rules and fail to assert your authority either from fear, lack of confidence or indifference, you are being unfair to the rest of the team as well as to the management of the salon.

There are times when a manager has not only to interpret the company's rules and procedures but to enforce them as well. People at work are fulfilling a contract with their employers which gives both sides privileges and obligations. These are worked out as a set of rules of behaviour which may be partly written, partly verbal. It is essential that you, as the manager, know these rules for you will have to act as an umpire or referee to see that they are observed. This does not mean that you have to be heavy-handed and constantly pointing the finger or taking disciplinary action. Indeed, you will soon be in trouble with managers and staff and demotivate people if you do. If a breach of discipline is serious, or is an open challenge to your authority, then you have no alternative but to act firmly. If the problem or issue is outside your experience or competence you will need to refer it upwards to your immediate superior. On every occasion it is important for you to be seen to be fair and impartial. The chances are that the rest of the team will then support you.

The following action should be taken:

(1) Make sure that every member of the team pulls his or her weight.
(2) If there is a breach of discipline don't tell staff off in front of the others but do it privately.
(3) Try to find out the reason for what has gone wrong, avoid speculation, and give fair warning of any steps you intend to take.
(4) Refer upwards any difficulty if it is beyond your competence or experience.
(5) Be seen to be fair and impartial.

### 4.1.5 *Manager as counsellor*

As leader of the team, you must expect people to come to you for advice. In fact, you should be worried if they don't. It may not always be convenient or easy but it is an obligation of your position as well as an act of friendship. Being prepared to listen and to act as a sounding board will often help them to put their problems into perspective. Your staff will come to value your advice if you can offer useful suggestions, such as putting them in touch with the appropriate support services, but not if you make unrealistic promises which are not followed up or try to solve their personal problems for them. Above all, what they tell you must be treated in confidence – they may talk about it to others but will not expect you to do so.

The following action should be taken:

(1) Take a personal interest in all your staff – don't say 'don't bring your

problems to work, pull yourself together'. Be available for advice and help.
(2) Be a good listener and try to offer helpful suggestions.
(3) Take the initiative in introducing staff to support services which may be helpful to them.
(4) When asked for advice concentrate on the facts not the emotions.
(5) Keep your counselling confidential.

### 4.1.6 *The manager as worker*

On the one hand it is important that you should be seen to be doing a reasonable portion of productive work, and that your standards should be as high as the staff's to set an example, e.g. quality haircuts, offering good service, treating the client civilly (even if they have been coming to you for 20 years), dressing the part, selling profitable services and generally setting an example. On the other hand, it is just as important to share out the key work, particularly the new clients, so that everyone had some inducement to get on with their part of the job.

There is a balance between being prepared to shoulder responsibility for the whole team of which you are a working member and ensuring that you delegate sufficient work so that you don't put yourself in the position of doing everything yourself while the staff sit and drink coffee in the staff room. Delegating always has a risk factor to it but it does not mean to say that we should not give staff responsibility. Being allowed to practise and make mistakes is one way to learn. The role of the manager is to ensure through training and good communication skills that the staff are allowed to develop at the pace that is right for them.

The following action should be taken:

(1) Learn to delegate while doing a fair share of the work yourself
(2) See that your standards set an example to the team
(3) Give credit where it is due
(4) Remember, you are responsible for your whole team's efforts

As a manager there is a lot to think about. You have to be a leader, communicator, trainer, umpire, counsellor and worker. Watching your team grow and develop so that they take responsibility for achieving goals and help to identify the problems as well as produce the solutions is one of the most rewarding aspects of managing people. We must therefore remember the following points:

- Set and maintain standards for the team by giving them clearly defined job descriptions and levels of authority.
- Train them to carry out their duties effectively at the speed and pace that is right for them.
- Be loyal to management and staff.
- Make sure everyone knows what is happening within the company and why.
- Listen to the team's views.
- Face problems before they get out of hand.
- Be firm but fair and try to understand the other person's point of view.
- Be responsible for the team's performance.

## 4.2 Communication

Communication, whether we are giving or receiving information, is the most fundamental skill that we must learn if we wish to be successful as a trainee, stylist or manager. Everyone plays a role in communication from the most junior member of staff to the manager or salon owner, making the salon function smoothly, efficiently and professionally. The process begins every time we have contact with a client or potential client, whether it is by telephone or in person.

Communication – what is it? The word 'communication' means to impart, transmit or share information. That means to give or to make known to people what it is they need to know. It also means to transmit information by the best possible method which will be explained later in this chapter.

### 4.2.1 *Why is communication important?*

Communication, if used positively, can help us to:

- Communicate with staff
- Communicate with superiors
- Communicate with clients
- Resolve conflict with staff and clients

*Negative communication* can easily take control if we become emotional in a situation. This in turn creates misunderstanding so that the relationship between staff, superiors and clients breaks down. Nothing is ever achieved from argument because the situation gets out of control. When we are emotional we do not hear what is being said and often our minds are already made up about the situation or the people. For example, if we do not like someone, then we are much harder on them or we look for the bad points in that particular person. Negative communication means that we will fail to understand our client's needs which, in turn, means that we will fail to offer the services of our salon. This has a direct effect upon everything within the salon. It can affect the amount of commission we earn or whether a client returns. It can prevent the business from growing and prospering. It can affect our image so that people feel we do not care about them, usually because we are too wrapped up in our thoughts or problems of the day.

*Positive communication* will therefore help us to reduce the day to day stress and pressure of working in the salon because we understand clearly what people want from us, or what we want from them.

Information, ideas, attitudes and knowledge must be freely interchanged within any salon if we want everyone to achieve their goals and for the salon to operate efficiently. The reasons for communication are:

(1) To share information with employees whether they are trainees, stylists, receptionists or managers
(2) To issue instructions to ensure co-operation and motivation so that staff know what is going on
(3) To establish positive behaviour in an informal working atmosphere
(4) To promote training and education – if we cannot communicate how can we train our staff?
(5) To ensure that problems within the salon are identified and dealt with swiftly

Effective communication is important to ensure that the manager or salon owner gives instructions which are:

- Relevant to the situation
- Communicated in a clear manner
- Understood by the receiver
- Acted upon

This involves the manager or salon owner satisfying the following conditions:

- Be clear as to what you wish to communicate.
- Consider the person to whom you are communicating.
- Use the most effective means of communication to fit the person and the situation.
- Transmit the information at the most appropriate time.
- Try to ensure that your communication has been understood and that the necessary action will be taken.

This means being sensitive to the ability of the person to take in the amount of information you give them. Watch for the following points:

(1) *The amount of information* – information is more effective in small doses, in a logical order rather than large quantities so that it can be readily absorbed.
(2) *Speed of assimilation* – this will vary according to the nature of the information and the receiver. Just because we are in a rush does not mean to say that by passing the information on quickly the receiver will absorb it.
(3) *New information* – this is only meaningful if the brain is also able to associate it with existing knowledge and experience. For example, young people have different life experiences than those of forty plus.
(4) *Interest* – people do not readily absorb information if they are not interested. Where possible, the method of communication should appeal to more than one sense.
(5) *Memory* – communicate the information in such a way that it will be remembered. Use examples and illustrations that will conjure up mental pictures or funny sayings in people's minds, e.g. if we build our people, our people will build our business.

### 4.2.2 The process of communication

When we communicate we go through a number of processes in giving information and receiving it (see Fig. 4.1). During this process we often create different barriers on different occasions or in different situations but once we are aware of what they are, then we can decide what we must do to communicate effectively all the time.

*Message*

When communicating we must first of all ask ourselves what we wish to achieve – in other words, what is the goal?

If our thoughts are jumbled then the message will be jumbled. There is no computerised sorting system between the brain and the mouth that will put it into a logical sequence. Many hairdressers often say 'I know what I feel but

**Fig. 4.1** The
process of
communication.

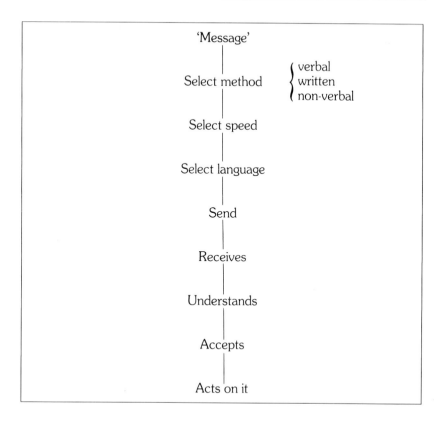

I have difficulty in expressing myself!' An effective way of describing the message is to jot down on a piece of paper what it is we are trying to achieve. When we see all the information written down it often helps us to clarify what we are trying to say and the order in which we say it. It is essential that we give people information in a logical sequence otherwise we will leave people more confused than when we started.

*Method*

Once we have decided upon the message we must then decide upon the best possible medium to use to communicate the message. There are three methods or channels of communication:

(1) *Verbal*

Verbal communication means to speak. The advantage of verbal communication is that it is quick and personalised. When we speak to people on a one-to-one basis face to face we can watch for the reaction to the message showing whether it has been received, accepted and understood.

The disadvantage of the spoken word is that we tend to forget some of the information that has been given. Most people take in approximately 40 per cent of the information particularly when the message is complicated, is new information or they are inexperienced in the area or subject of the message.

The other disadvantage of verbal communication is that there is no action replay. We cannot press a button and remind ourselves of what has just been said.

(2) *Written*

The written word as a method of communication has a number of advantages and disadvantages. We can use sketches, drawings, diagrams and photographs as a method to reinforce the message. We can absorb the information at our own pace and go back over what might have been forgotten, to reinforce the message.

The disadvantage of written communication is that it is often impersonal. There is usually no opportunity to question what the message means and its implications or to receive or observe the reaction of the person receiving it. Written communication should be used if the message is:

- Important
- Complicated
- New information or ideas which will take time to absorb

(3) *Non-verbal*

Non-verbal communication is the method we use to convey information through either our bodily or facial expressions. The advantage of non-verbal communication is that it is quiet and visual. Many people who work in hairdressing learn by visual things, by watching as opposed to reading or listening. The advantage of non-verbal communication is that we learn by example, by watching or seeing something demonstrated.

| Type | Advantages | Disadvantages | Other comments |
|---|---|---|---|
| (1) *Verbal* Talking, meetings etc. | Quick and straightforward. Cheap. Feedback immediately possible. No distortion if direct. | Requires speaker to be skilful in how to communicate. Choice of language, style etc. | Practice two-way communication *especially* listening skills. |
| (2) *Written* Noticeboards, letters, memos, handbooks etc. | More permanent record. Can be proven to have been sent. Usually more explicit and needs to be kept simple. | Slow – takes time. Expensive. May not be seen/received. | Use to support verbal communication as a permanent record etc. |
| (3) *Non-verbal* Signals | Secretive. Visual and can be done where there is much noise. Difficult to falsify. | Easily misunderstood. Ambiguous. | Use to check for effectiveness of verbal communication and to verify response. |

**Fig. 4.2** Advantages and disadvantages of different forms of communication.

The disadvantage of non-verbal communication is that it is often misunderstood. We misunderstand others and they misunderstand us. It is very easy to jump to conclusions as to what we think someone's facial or bodily expressions mean. If we see someone laughing at a party are they laughing because they are happy, nervous, or drunk? It could mean any of these things.

To summarise on the three methods of communication we recommend that as many methods as possible are used to communicate and reinforce the message, particularly when the information is new, complicated or controversial (see Fig. 4.2).

### Speed

By this we mean the speed at which people can take in new information or how quickly we tend to talk. The speed must vary according to the kind of information and the person who will be receiving it.

We also need to remember the size of the audience. One-to-one conversations mean that we can speak at the speed that the other person can take in the information. Ten people – we must speak at the speed everyone can understand. One hundred people – we must speak as if there is a pause between every word. Finally, we must vary the light and shade in the voice – speaking in a monotone makes it very difficult for people to concentrate and receive the message.

### Language

This area is of particular importance because hairdressers and manufacturers are very good at talking in a language and jargon that clients do not understand. The term 'acid balanced perm' has quite a different meaning to a hairdresser than it does to a client. This is just as bad as the man in the shop selling us a camera who talks about shutter speeds or a car salesman who talks about front wheel drive. We must always remember the person receiving the message and pitch our language and terminology at the level that the receiver of the message can understand.

### Send

Once we have mastered these five areas of communication when giving information to people then we must check that the message has been understood.

### Receiving information

We can check that information has been received by the receiver's body language, facial expressions and the questions they ask. For example, nodding the head, smiling, leaning forward in the chair and eye contact all indicate that the message is being received.

### Understanding the message

Receiving the message clearly is not the same as understanding what the message means. We must explore this area with the right questioning techniques. Do not take at face value nods, smiles and eye contact as meaning the message has been understood. Use open and probing questions to ensure that it has (see Section 3.8.2 on Questioning techniques).

*Accepted*

Understanding the message does not mean that we have agreed with it! Listen carefully to the way in which people respond. Does the 'yes' mean 'no' and the 'no' mean 'yes'? Sometimes the receiver may say 'yes' they understand and agree but there are tell-tale signs which show us that they do not. This is where our listening skills must come into play in terms of asking open questions and listening carefully to the replies.

We must *look* for signs of disagreement in the staff's facial expressions or body language. *Listen* to the way in which they reply and if we are in doubt we should *explore* further by asking open and probing questions.

There are other reasons why the receiver may not accept what we have to say. They could be:

- They do not like us or the position we hold
- They may have a grudge towards us **over** an event in the past
- They may have problems not connected with the salon
- They lack experience and knowledge

If any of the above happen we cannot off-load responsibility but we must try harder to get the receiver to accept what we have been saying.

*Act upon it*

Once the message has been received, understood and accepted there is still no guarantee at this stage that the receiver will put the request into action or operation. There could be a number of reasons for this:

(1) We may not have explained how important it is to do it now.
(2) We may have given them several other instructions all at the same time.
(3) The receiver's priority may not be ours unless we have clearly identified the order in which we would like them carried out.

### 4.2.3 Listening

There are also a number of barriers to listening effectively and once we identify them, we can look at methods of improving our ability to listen more carefully.

*Self-consciousness*

If we are too concerned about the way we look or how we may appear particularly if we are in a new job and want to impress someone, we often fail to hear what is being said. We can overcome this by admitting that we feel self-conscious or concerned about the impression we might make. This often helps to change the atmosphere.

*The long speech*

Some people seem to take forever to make their point. The trouble with long speeches is that the listener tends to lose parts of what is being said – particularly the middle parts. Overcome this by interrupting the speaker if you feel you have lost the thread. Summarise what you think you may have heard and check it out with the sender of the message.

*Repetition*

There are some people who switch into the same groove of the record with certain people or situations so that the receiver of the message switches off. If we do this we must ensure that we 're-package' the message on different occasions so that people start to listen.

*Dislike*

If we dislike the message or the person this may arouse anger or hostility. We need to be aware of our feelings and, if appropriate, share them with the other person. Concentrate on what is being said and do not take the message personally.

*Noise*

Noise may prevent the message from being heard, either by drowning the message or causing concentration or attention to be shifted elsewhere. Remove obvious distractions such as telephones and interruptions.

*Assumptions*

We may be familiar with the task or information we wish to communicate and often assume that the person receiving the information has the same level of knowledge and experience as us. We tend to miss out vital clues and links and jump from A to Z and assume the person receiving the message understands all the connecting bits in between. Remember the age, knowledge and experience of the person to whom you are talking – particularly in young people.

*Tiredness*

Tiredness tends to make people switch off or become easily distracted when listening. We can avoid this by ensuring that important messages or conversations are restricted to times or periods of the day when they are less tired, stressed or pressurised. The result of tiredness is often emotion which creeps in and creates a barrier in communicating or listening to information.

In conclusion, there is more to giving and receiving information than meets the eye. If we identify at each stage or step where communication may break down then we can take the appropriate action to improve communications within our salon.

## 4.3 Motivation

There has been more research and interest in motivation than in any other area of managing people because, clearly, motivation holds the key to successful salon management. Motivated staff work hard, attract and keep clients, give good service, and are loyal. On the other hand, demotivated staff create a bad image and can be lazy which in turn can affect other staff. Motivation for the owner or manager is vital to get the business forging ahead and to keep it there.

When we discuss motivation we are usually seeking the answers to two questions:

(1) Why do people work?
(2) Why do some people work harder than others?

It is the experience of all of us that two almost identical people will be differently motivated – one requiring constant pushing to achieve, the other almost having to be held back.

What does motivating staff mean? In the next section we will look at the theories of motivation and apply them to salon management. An interesting point to look at is what demotivates staff. What makes them continually

**Fig. 4.3** Ten guaranteed ways to demotivate your staff.

(1) Never praise them or thank them for their efforts. After all, they get paid.
(2) Tell them as little as possible about the business, its problems and the future. After all, it's none of their business and they are not interested.
(3) If they are a few minutes late occasionally or even just on time, make a point of checking or telling them. You can't trust staff.
(4) Always tell them off in public, especially in front of colleagues or customers. It puts them in their place.
(5) If they are female, keep chatting them up, offering to take them out, and fondling them. After all they really like it and they are your employees.
(6) If they do something well or special, make sure you get the credit and not them. You're more important than they are.
(7) If they come to you with personal problems, do your best not to listen. If you have to listen, say helpful things like:

• Don't bring your personal problems to work.
• Pull yourself together, woman.
• Grow up!

You must never show any sympathy or understanding – life is tough!

(8) Keep changing the rules, i.e. what you expect them to do, but don't tell them. It keeps them on their toes.
(9) Always assume they are wrong without finding out the facts. After all, you are too busy to play detective and they'll only cover for one another.
(10) Pay your favourites more than the rest of them and treat them well – after all they are the best and most reliable staff.

switch off at work? In Fig. 4.3 we have listed ten guaranteed ways to demotivate your staff. After looking at this list can you say in all honesty that you have never done any of these things? If you have, they are the first things to cut out if you wish to improve motivation. Exercise 4.1 is a motivation questionnaire to look at your beliefs. What does it show you about yourself? After completing this think about what motivates you and secondly, what motivates your staff. What you think motivates them and what they think motivates them will probably be quite different.

### Exercise 4.1 Motivation questionnaire

If you feel the following statement is generally true mark T, if you feel it is generally false mark F and if you think it is neither or you cannot answer mark N.

(1) It would help if people showed more interest in their jobs. _____

(2) I can offer no real incentives if people improve so I don't really bother. _____

(3) I find I need to punish more than praise or reward staff. _____

(4) Staff feel they do not get enough reward already for the effort they put in. _____

(5) I don't review staff performance, i.e. tell them how they are doing, very often because I am too busy. _____

(6) I am not able to support the staff as much as I would like as I have a heavy workload myself. _____

(7) People have to work a lot of hours and hard to earn a proper wage. _____

(8) People wouldn't welcome more challenge in their jobs. _____

(9) The business pays less than competition and some staff are unhappy about that. _____

(10) I don't believe staff are committed either to the job or to the salon. _____

(11) There is not a very happy atmosphere in the salon. _____

(12) There seem to be lots of niggling small arguments going on here. _____

(13) We find it hard to attract and keep good staff in the salon. _____

(14) Staff often seem to play up and cause disagreements over very minor issues. _____

(15) I don't feel staff really understand or sympathise with my problems as an owner/manager. _____

Add up the total number of  Ts
Add ½ point for each        N
Score 0 for                 ⊦
Then total your score

Minimum = 0   Maximum = 15

Scoring

More than 10   You have serious problems and a lot of hard work to do if you are to change things.

7–10          There are certainly a number of areas in which you can improve.

Less than 6    You seem to have a well-run business unless you have not noticed the problems.

### 4.3.1 The theory of motivation

There has been more written about human motivation than probably any other area of management – literally hundreds of articles. We have prepared here a brief summary on the main theories of motivation but sources of further information are listed in the Appendix. We have summarised the theories into the following three areas:

(1)  Basic ideas and conclusions of motivational theory.
(2)  Application to the hairdressing industry.
(3)  Implications for action.

The approaches to motivation we discuss here are those of Taylor, Mayo, Maslow, Herzberg, McClelland, Vroom and Goldthorpe. These are by no means the only views but they are the most widely accepted and seem to have the most relevance for managing hairdressing businesses.

*Taylor (principles of scientific management)*

Taylor described a number of factors which influenced successful performance:

(1)  Choose the best man for the job (selection).
(2)  Show him the best method for doing the job (training).
(3)  Give him the proper tools for the job.
(4)  Relate his pay to his performance or productivity directly. Assuming (1) to (3) are observed, then by relating an individual's pay *directly* to his performance, e.g. commission or bonus, this will produce the necessary motivation.

Thus, Taylor's ideas were the founding ones of many bonus systems still existing today and see staff as motivated by *money* or economic factors primarily.

The implications for hairdressing are that if you are using a *bonus system* then money (pay) must be within the control of the staff, i.e. they must be able to affect their own earnings. In many salons this is just not true, since clientele are fixed and some days are slack. We explain later how payment systems can be designed to get around this.

### Mayo (Hawthorne studies)

Mayo was examining the effects of a large number of factors on work output, e.g. rest pauses, lighting, supervision etc.

What was found was that staff's individual motivations were modified or affected by the work-group or team in a given situation and that this force could be a positive one or a negative one from management's point of view depending on circumstances.

This is clearly relevant in managing a salon as there is clearly a *team* in that:

(1) Staff are physically close together
(2) They have common goals and objectives
(3) They are interdependent
(4) They form (working) relationships and interact together continuously

The implications of this are that we must consider the effects of changes on salon staff *both* as individuals *and* as a group and that efforts to improve the image of that group and enhance its status etc. are likely to be useful. On the other hand, things which damage the harmony or image of the group, e.g. inconsistency and unfairness, may well lead to demotivation and poor output.

### Maslow (a theory of human motivation)

Maslow wrote from the view of a developmental psychologist and was interested in the fundamental needs which people had. He saw those needs as developmental and hierarchical, i.e. some basic and others high-level which emerged when the lower-level needs were satisfied. Figure 4.4 illustrates this principle.

**Fig. 4.4** Maslow's hierarchy of needs.

| | | | |
|---|---|---|---|
| (1) Physiological (Basic needs) | Food Sleep | Water Sex | Oxygen Warmth |
| (2) Security (Need to feel secure and safe) | Safety Security Continuity | | Predictability Comfort |
| (3) Social (Need to belong and have friends) | Love Friends Affiliation | | Affection Belonging |
| (4) Esteem (Need for respect and to be respected) | Self respect Respect from others Recognition | | Pride Status Achievement |
| (5) Self-actualisation (Ultimate realisation of all your potential as a person) | Being Development Personal fulfilment 100% + | Growth | |

Maslow's view was that once lower-level needs had been satisfied, then higher-level needs could emerge. Thus for Maslow:

(1) Behaviour attempts to satisfy needs.
(2) Satisfied needs do not motivate.

The implications of all this are to know for all our staff which of their needs are fulfilled and to note that when certain problems arise – marital or relationship break-up or redundancy – we may 'slip down the hierarchy' and safety/security and social needs become important. Youngsters are likely to be satisfying social or ego needs whereas older people may well be concentrating on higher-level needs. Finally, if lower-levels become problematical, e.g. low income or financial difficulties, then these may (temporarily) halt the seeking of the higher-level needs until these lower-level ones are met.

*Herzberg (motivator – hygiene theory)*

Herzberg researched engineers/scientists to find out what turned them on at work and what turned them off.

He identified two kinds of factors operating at work: those which cause satisfaction at work and hence (says Herzberg) motivate people, called *motivators* or *satisfiers*, and a second group called *hygiene factors* or *dissatisfiers* which cause dissatisfaction and demotivate staff. The other point he made was that by removing the dissatisfiers you do not get motivation, only the motivators can do that. Conversely, the motivation effects can be modified if the hygiene factors go wrong. Figure 4.5 shows the two sets of factors.

We must explain the place of salary. Herzberg argues that pay *does not in itself motivate* but rather if people feel underpaid it *certainly does demotivate*. An interesting result Herzberg also noted was that increases in pay have a short-term effect which falls off as we adjust to the new income level.

The implications for hairdressing then are that we should try to get the hygiene factors 'right', i.e. remove the demotivating factors, then attempt to

**Fig. 4.5**
Herzberg's
motivator –
hygiene theory.

Motivators
(1)   Achievement
(2)   Recognition
(3)* Work itself (interesting or stimulating)
(4)* Responsibility
(5)* Advancement
* Important for long-term effect

Hygiene factors
(1) Company policy and rules
(2) Supervision
(3) Salary
(4) Interpersonal relations
(5) Working conditions

build into jobs as many of the motivators as possible. This process is called *job enrichment*.

### McClelland (achievement motivation)

McClelland notes that some people are highly motivated by a need to achieve, to be successful – he calls it 'NACH'. Not everyone has it and different cultures have it more than others. Achievement-motivated individuals want:

* Improvement
* Performance
* Challenge etc

They set their personal targets for accomplishment high and strive to achieve them. They constantly want review, feedback, and to know how well they are doing.

McClelland also notices that this can be learned by using four points:

(1) Teach people to think, talk and act achievement.
(2) Stimulate people to set well planned targets or goals.
(3) Help people to become more aware of themselves.
(4) Create a team spirit by sharing hopes, fears, successes and failures. The evidence in many areas was 'it works'.

The implications here are exciting. You can build success. You can change motivation in staff by building (1) to (4) above into your staff training. But it takes time and it's hard work! But it's worth it. Thus we have to work at building a real functioning team.

### Vroom (expectancy theory)

Expectancy theory takes a slightly different approach and sees motivation as a logical choice among alternatives. Thus people consider what will be the result and is it worth it (see Fig. 4.6). Suppose you are asked to work hard in exchange for a bonus. Whether you will or not depends upon:

* How much you want the bonus
* Whether you believe the extra work will bring the return

Notice that the expectancy and valence are individual things based on

**Fig. 4.6** Expectancy theory.

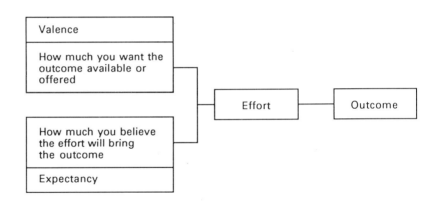

personal views and experience. Thus, if your experience is that you never get the return for hard work, even if you still want it your motivation will go down.

This is particularly useful when designing payment systems. If you want pay (or anything else, for that matter) to motivate you must meet four conditions:

(1) Employees must expect effort to be worthwhile.
(2) They must believe results will bring the reward.
(3) They must want the reward.
(4) They must want it badly enough to make the effort worthwhile.

### Goldthorpe (affluent worker in the class structure)

This last approach is not a theory of motivation as such but simply notes that for many people work is not important in itself but is simply a means to an end, e.g. money. Thus, for some people work is only important in that it allows them to earn the money to do what they really want to do – whatever that is, e.g. bring up a family, go out with friends.

This is called the 'instrumental approach' – it is important in that people with this kind of orientation are not motivated by job enrichment and this has serious implications for such programmes if significant numbers of people are instrumental in orientation. They will be more interested in time off, etc. However, they can be motivated by exchanging say 'time off' for hard work or something of that kind. One example often quoted in the hairdressing area is the single parent who, in exchange for being able to take odd days off and work school hours, will be a very 'motivated' worker and 'produce the goods'.

### Summary

The various theories of motivation have in common the view that people *do* things in attempting to satisfy personal goals and objectives (what ever these are) and that motivation is about trying to allow people to achieve these through the work that they do in your business.

People's needs are very different and recent research has looked at the way that even for the same person they change over time from young single to married to married with children to retired etc. Money is clearly not the only motivator although it does play an important role; some of the other motivators (see Herzberg's list) can be built into jobs by the process of job enrichment.

People's experiences affect the extent to which various rewards motivate them, and these change as they gather new experiences, and rewards achieve new levels of importance to them.

Thus in order to motivate staff we need to:

(1) Know as much about what 'makes them tick' as possible and hence their needs and orientation to work
(2) Examine the extent to which we can help them achieve at least some of these in the work place
(3) Try to remove the obstacles for motivation (hygiene factors) to ensure maximum benefits
(4) Keep in mind the importance of group motivation as well as individual motivation.

For many people the challenge of the job itself is important and we can encourage people to want to achieve by careful development and nurturing.

We must attempt to ensure people are clear as to what their efforts will bring and that expectations will be met and they will not feel hard done by.

In conclusion, then, motivation of most staff is possible by paying attention to the points discussed above provided we try to remove (and do not add to!) the possible sources of demotivation we explored earlier.

### 4.3.2 The practical application

*Putting theory into practice – a three-part plan to get it right*

In this section we need to examine an outline plan for effective motivation which will be achieved by the following three approaches:

(1) Managing staff properly and getting communications and relationships right
(2) Creating an environment in which staff can develop and grow and achieve their own needs
(3) Designing an effective payment system to motivate staff and to ensure a fair return for their efforts

We maintain that these three areas, if correctly organised, will create a climate in which there is motivation of staff and a successful business for you. One in which the staff get a fair and just return for their efforts. It is often said that you get the kind of staff you deserve and the staff problems you deserve. Salon owners and managers who are fair and honest and treat staff and clients well generally do well. Those who are greedy, dishonest and manipulative may do well for a time but eventually things will catch up with them and they will experience real problems.

There is no simple magic formula for success. Managing staff requires people skills, an empathy and willingness to see their problems as people and a desire to help them achieve. This must not be at the expense of a successful and profitable business. The two can work together so that everyone, staff, management and clients, can benefit.

In order to examine the question of whether you and your staff have motivational problems we have designed a questionnaire to test whether there is room for improvement or not (Exercise 4.2). Check if your staff have the right attitudes to each other, to you and to your clients. The signs of poor morale and motivation are complex and the methods to improve them follow in the next section.

*Managing by motivation*

So how do we effectively manage staff? The key is to action the following areas:

(1) The staff must know exactly what is expected of them – the standards required and the rules and procedures of the Company.
(2) They must be involved in the setting of those standards or at least have the opportunity of discussing them with you.
(3) They must understand the goals and objectives of the business – where it is going, why and how they fit into it and what they must do in order to help achieve the objectives.

(4) They need to feel a part of that business and to feel comfortable so that they can raise problems as they see them without fear of criticism or aggravation. They need to know that they will be consulted and informed when changes take place that directly affect them.

(5) They need to know that as a result of keeping their part of the bargain you will keep yours and that they will receive a fair return for their efforts; that they will be treated fairly and equally as human beings not hair cutting machines, so that they can give a proper service to clients and earn respect and self esteem for themselves.

Figure 4.7 details a checklist for effective management in hairdressing.

*Setting standards*

We cannot stress how important it is to ensure that there are proper job

**Fig. 4.7** A checklist for effective management.

(1) (With the person involved) *Develop a simple outline of the job and key tasks to be performed.* This can apply to an individual job or to a complete salon. It should include a simple statement of what people are to do, what authority they have in doing it, and what their relationships with other people are.

(2) (With the person involved) *Develop a simple statement of the results that will be considered satisfactory.* There are many activities for which, at first, it seems impossible to develop standards of performance. However, discussion of them in a sincere attempt to develop standards will often produce definite and acceptable objectives.

(3) (With the person involved) *At regular intervals, check actual performance against the standards that have been set.* If the supervisor is to plan his activities, he must know how big a gap there is between what is being done and what should be done. This should be checked in terms of individual and group attainment.

(4) (With the person involved) *Make a list of corrective actions necessary to improve performance where needed.* An individual cannot develop into a better worker unless he is continuously increasing his skill, gaining knowledge, changing his habits and assuming constructive attitudes. A manager should know where improvement is needed.

(5) (With the person involved) *Select the best sources from which he can obtain help and information.* Sources can be divided into four categories: the immediate manager, the other individuals in the organisation, people outside the organisation who could be brought in, and outside sources of help to which the individual concerned could be referred. These sources should be considered in that order and the one which is most advantageous selected.

(6) (With the person involved) *A time should be set aside in advance for supplying the help and information that is needed.* If we do not plan in advance, the time can be made available only through disrupting the work of the salon. It is of little use to go to all the trouble of deciding what should be done, analysing what has been done, and determining what action is needed, if no action is taken.

descriptions and written staff rules and regulations with clearly defined standards for all. These standards must be encouraged. Every time you make an exception or ask the staff to drop their standards you erode them. Every time you fail to 'pull up' staff who break the rules, you erode the rules. *Consistency is vital.* We have detailed this in greater depth in Section 3.3 on job descriptions but need to add that the standard of performance must be the same for each person who carries out this job. Each stylist must have the same standard of performance in terms of the number of clients they are expected to cover each week if they have had the same amount of experience. A standard is not the same as a goal. A standard is the acceptable minimum requirement to be successful at doing the job. Goals or targets are the level towards which they are expected to work. The goal or target will be dependent upon their experience, the type of clients and the range of services offered to clients.

The standards must take account of:

- The level of training or experience of staff
- The volume of business being done (as this is often dependent upon promotional activity of the salon)
- A reasonable day's work taking into account client cancellations
- The incentive or method of payment

The standards should be reviewed regularly and changed if necessary.

Staff need to have copies or at least access to this information because, if they do not know what is expected of them they cannot meet the requirements. Staff should have regular reviews or appraisals and these should be a basis for discussions and improvement, not simply criticism.

Staff need to feel they know what is going on, to feel part of the business. In particular, they need to know the opportunities for promotion or advancement, any future training or new experience they will have or even any additional responsibilities that they may get in the future.

They also need to feel that they too can make a contribution to improvement and that they can make suggestions about improvements. Have you ever asked them for their views? Do you really listen to their problems? Do you really care about what they think or feel? If you do not, then you cannot really blame them for not being sympathetic to your problems or difficulties.

Communication is a vital part of this process. Staff need to know what is going on, especially when it affects them.

*Creating the right environment*

It is very difficult to pin-point exactly what is the right environment for staff but certainly we should aim for the following:

(1) An atmosphere of openness and trust
(2) Minimal conflict
(3) Clear objectives, goals and standards
(4) Clear lines of responsibility and authority
(5) Staff who are keen to take on responsibility
(6) A feeling of support, comfort and teamwork
(7) Opportunities for responsibility for staff
(8) Loyalty to the company, staff, products and services
(9) Adequate communication of key issues

(10) Friendliness between staff
(11) Low staff turnover (staff leaving)
(12) High staff productivity and morale
(13) A sense of competition with other salons

In our experience, it is often the management's style or lack of expertise which gives rise to problems of motivation. Exercise 4.2 is a questionnaire upon the climate or environment of the salon. Ask the staff to complete this questionnaire anonymously. The answers may surprise you.

---

**Exercise 4.2  Climate analysis**
Answer the following statements about this salon by marking each question according to your answer. If statement is:

| | | |
|---|---|---|
| Always true | mark | T |
| Quite often true | mark | O |
| Sometimes true | mark | S |
| Very seldom true | mark | V |
| Never true | mark | N |

(1) There are good working relationships between the senior and junior staff here.  _____

(2) This salon feels nice to work in.  _____

(3) You don't feel you will get chewed up if you make the odd mistake.  _____

(4) You daren't argue with the manager/owner's decisions.  _____

(5) You get fairly rewarded for what you do here.  _____

(6) Everyone is clear what is required of them here.  _____

(7) The place is full of rules and regulations – you don't know which way to turn.  _____

(8) You are encouraged to show initiative and make decisions yourself here.  _____

(9) I feel loyal to this salon and never say bad things about it.  _____

(10) I think I would leave this salon if I could get more money elsewhere.  _____

*Scoring*
For questions 1, 2, 3, 5, 6, 7, 8, 9 score:
  5 for T
  4 for O
  3 for S
  2 for V
  1 for N

For questions 4, 10 score:
  1 for T
  2 for V
  3 for S
  4 for V
  5 for N

Minimum score = 10   Maximum score = 50
Add up to get total score.

Interpretations
Under 25   You have serious problems and you should examine them carefully. Look at what your staff are telling you.
25–35      Things are not too bad but there is room for improvement. Start on the worst areas.
Over 35    You have got a good environment. Look at the areas which still need improvement and work on them.

---

Now you have an indication of the staff's feelings about the climate or atmosphere in the salon – check your own management expertise by considering the questions below:

(1) Am I clear about my own responsibility and level of authority?
(2) Am I clear about the objectives of my salon and the group as a whole?
(3) Have I worked out a plan of action for reaching these goals/objectives?
(4) Can the jobs of the staff be re-constructed to get better results?
(5) Are the physical working conditions, layout, equipment and lighting right for the job?
(6) Does everyone know exactly what their job is? Has each member of staff clearly defined targets and performance standards agreed with them? Have I the same with my boss?
(7) Does everyone know to whom they should report?
(8) Has anyone too many people reporting to them which makes them manage inefficiently? If so, can this responsibility be shared with another?
(9) Is the line of authority clear for each member of staff?
(10) Are there any gaps in the abilities of the staff? If so, am I taking steps to fill them by training, by additional staff or the use of specialists?
(11) Am I aware of how I and my staff spend our time? Is it the best way? Are our priorities right?
(12) Have I achieved the tasks set 12 months ago? If not, why not?
(13) Does my own work and behaviour set the best possible example to the group?

If the answer to any of the above questions is no then you clearly have areas for improvement.

*Guidelines for self-improvement*

We offer some guidelines on how to improve yourself as a manager or salon owner in three key areas:

(1) New ideas
(2) Personal conduct
(3) Self-development

*New ideas*
- Look around at your salon internally and externally.
- Look at competitors' activities.
- Read magazines, books and newspapers for ideas.
- Don't jump to conclusions about staff (see Communication section on non-verbal behaviour).
- Listen to staff's and clients' needs even when you are harassed or tired.

*Personal conduct*
- A manager or salon owner cannot forget his or her position – be friendly but not over familiar.
- Do not invite gossip by your lifestyle because you will not get the respect you would like. This is particularly so if you are emotionally involved with members of your staff.
- Be discreet in your working environment and personal life.
- Do not talk over your personal problems with the staff.
- Do not have favourites within the salon.
- Do not have special friendships with superiors.
- Do not be over familiar at social gatherings and only go to them occasionally, not every Friday night tap-dancing on the pub bar!
- We all like to be liked but our staff expect a code of conduct from us.
- Respect does not necessarily come from our status – we have to earn it.

*Self-development*
- Mixing with people from a similar environment is good as it stops us from being insular.
- Develop yourself by cultivating other interests outside hairdressing. All work and no play makes for very boring people!
- Try and identify your faults always and work to eliminate them.

### 4.3.3 Designing an effective payment system

There is probably no area of management activity that causes more difficulty than the determination of pay. In our research and experience in hairdressing it was the single most common cause of annoyance, demotivation and staff leaving the industry.

The range of payment methods is incredible from straight salary, to bonus payments and a wide range of commission schemes from the simple to the complex. We have found many fair, honest and legal pay schemes and some which were blatantly unfair, immoral and illegal in operation.

In order to develop and maintain an effective payment system it is necessary to:

- Understand the basic principles
- Appreciate the range of options available
- Select the best system for your salon
- Introduce changes carefully after planning
- Monitor the effectiveness of the system

There are two basic approaches to wage systems within the hairdressing industry. The first is payment based on the time worked, such as by the hour, week, month or year. The second is payment based on output or productivity. Both approaches can be used satisfactorily, depending upon the job in question. In practice, pay may be made up of both approaches. Look at the following list of factors regarding payment on the basis of time or output.

*Output/time factors*

(1) Individual output is distinct and clearly measurable.
(2) Concern with quality is less important than concern with quantity.
(3) Quantity is important.
(4) The work is standardised and delays are few.
(5) Supervision is spread amongst a number of staff.
(6) Supervisors know what constitutes a fair day's work.
(7) There is a sizeable relationship between effort and quantity of output.
(8) There are many interferences with work that are outside the control of the employee.
(9) There is little or no relationship between effort and output.
(10) Output is clearly under the control of the employee.

Ouput factors: numbers 3, 4, 7, 10.
Time factors: numbers 1, 2, 5, 6, 8, 9.

Most of the factors concerned with output are not true. In the strict sense, the stylist cannot control how hard he/she works without reducing standards and does not have the ability to generate new clients except in a limited way by personal reference from existing clients and looking after the ones already visiting the salon so that they return again. Salons have quiet days when clearly even if stylists tried to work hard they could not. This would suggest that a pure bonus system or commission scheme is incorrect and that a wage or guaranteed basic wage would be more appropriate.

There are, however, a number of areas where the stylist's expertise contributes to volume of clients:

(1) Client loyalty – new clients returning as regulars
(2) Selling retail products
(3) Selling technical services such as colours and perms

It is for this reason that we feel that some form of bonus system is required and would propose a system of part salary and part bonus as discussed later in this chapter.

Two further complications affect the calculations:

(1) Staff help each other, e.g. trainees wash hair for stylists
(2) The salon needs to be kept clean and tidy and staff need to be trained in all jobs which conventionally do not earn bonus or commission

What, therefore, should be the principles of a good scheme? We feel the following points must be taken into account for a scheme to work well:

(1) Pay must consistently relate to performance whether in terms of productivity or standards.
(2) The system must keep labour costs within reasonable limits – a maximum wage cost of 'productive staff' to turnover excluding VAT of 53 per cent including employer's National Insurance contributions.
(3) The system must be easily understood by staff.
(4) The system must not penalise trainees or inexperienced staff but must create sufficient differentials between them and experienced stylists.
(5) The system must ensure that there are no anomalies, e.g. inexperienced staff earning more than experienced stylists.
(6) The pay scheme should generate a salary roughly in line with competition.

(7) The system should have an in-built flexibility and the option of regular reviews.
(8) It should reward achievement as quickly as possible after results (e.g. not a bonus paid just on an annual basis).
(9) The pay scheme should be instrumental in:

- attracting staff
- keeping staff

(10) The system should be easily administered and not require excessive records or large amounts of paperwork.

*Which pay scheme?*

We suggest four approaches as the most useful to consider:

(1) A straight commission scheme (a percentage of turnover net of VAT) or a minimum wage whichever is the greater
(2) Group bonus scheme based on total turnover and proportioned by status and/or experience or volume
(3) A bonus system based on points of the individual or the salon group
(4) Straight salaries

*Straight commission scheme*

We have found this system to be the commonest method used for stylists with juniors/trainees paid a straight wage. It is problematical with many of the commission schemes currently running in the hairdressing industry, in that it is still possible to work very hard on some days yet get no bonus.

Some salons work the commission scheme on a daily basis but this can increase the wage costs although it does motivate staff. Many salons have complete sliding scales and different rates for new or regular clients which no one except the wages clerk understands.

A number of salons have pay schemes which do not have an added incentive to generate extra income as they are only paid the additional commission rate on the difference between the lower scale of earnings and the higher scale not the total amount.

*Group bonus scheme*

Another basic and simple system is to pay everyone a basic rate and calculate the bonus or commission as follows:

- Calculate the normal wages for staff based on the agreed wage.
- Calculate the percentage of turnover using average past takings less VAT.
- The total bonus is the difference between the figures.
- It is then shared out proportionally so that the manager, stylists, receptionists and juniors all have a share in the bonus scheme depending upon their status.

This system emphasises team effort and status of each staff member. It requires:

- An agreed basic rate not a minimum wage
- An agreed group bonus system

- An agreement as to what happens if they do not meet the bonus on a regular basis – this means that either management bears the cost and staff get basic pay or the shortfall is carried forward and deducted next time
- Historical wage data

The group bonus scheme is an effective and motivating system and has a number of benefits:

(1) It forces management to promote the business.
(2) It generates team effort.
(3) The most junior and inexperienced staff share in the success of the salon, e.g. trainees and receptionists.
(4) It eliminates prima donnas.
(5) It ensures management and receptionists fairly distribute new clients.
(6) It does not penalise long-standing stylists who tend to have a larger clientele of shampoo and sets or shampoo and blow dries and who have difficulty in increasing their maximum takings due to the lower price charged for these services.
(7) It is easy to administer.


*Points bonus system*

There are a wide range of methods and we outline only a few possibilities. Basically, for every client handled in any way points are awarded as follows:

- 1 point for reception
- 2 points for washing
- 3 points for cut and blow dry
- 1 point for retail sales

This can be extended to non-client activities, e.g.

- 5 points for washing the floor
- 8 points for training and so on

At the end of a given time period (weekly or monthly) the total points for all staff are calculated.

Points are valued at, say, 5p or whatever sum of money the salon can afford and wishes to place upon the work. This is to ascertain the bonus element. The difference between basic pay and the points system is the 'commission'.

Each member of staff would then get paid according to the points as follows:

| | |
|---|---|
| Staff member A | 1000 points |
| Staff member B | 600 points |
| Staff member C | 800 points |
| Staff member D | 600 points |
| | 3000 points |

Money available for bonus, say £150, therefore each point is worth 5p, therefore:

Staff member A receives £50
Staff member C receives £40
Staff members B and D receive £30 each

The staff receive this bonus as a monthly sum or in four weekly instalments over the next four weeks.

This scheme can be enhanced by introducing deductions for rule breaking or introducing extra points for extra things, e.g. promoting perms for one month would buy extra points. It does require openness and honesty in its administration and no favourites.

*Straight salary*

In this system we would recommend paying the straight salary every week or month regardless of turnover. This is a common method of payment in

**Fig. 4.8** Fringe benefits for hairdressers.

| Option | Net cost |
|---|---|
| (1) Products at cost or discount | Nil (reduces pilferage) |
| (2) Reduced prices for friends/relatives | Small (may bring in new clients) |
| (3) Free overalls/uniforms | Nominal if rental firm used |
| (4) Motor car | £3500 pa – becoming common practice in larger salon groups at management level |
| (5) Bus fares/travel expenses | Variable |
| (6) Dryers/combs etc. *free* | Can be expensive – better to sell at wholesale |
| (7) Subsidised pension schemes, particularly for managers | Unattractive to the young |
| (8) Luncheon vouchers | £3 pw per staff – staff from other industries like this a lot but very rarely used in the hairdressing industry |
| (9) Extra holidays with service | Nominal |
| (10) Own hair done free | Small |
| (11) Mortgages at attractive rates | Small if already negotiating with own financial suppliers |
| (12) Low cost rent or tied property over salons | Variable – depends on area and whether property could be used for other purposes |
| (13) Reduced rate package holidays | Variable depending upon local travel agent and personal connections |
| (14) Private medical insurance | Small – dependent upon size of company |

industry but it is difficult to change the motivation of staff with this method and we do not particularly recommend it for the hairdressing industry unless straight salaries are paid at senior management level.

An alternative to the straight salary could be to pay 90 per cent of salary each week and keep a monthly 10 per cent available as a discretionary bonus element which might then act as an incentive system.

### Conclusions

We have tried to illustrate briefly in this section the kinds of payment systems that can be used within your business. They are by no means the only ones – there are over 250 different types of pay schemes available.

We would recommend that this is one area where professional advice from management consultants is essential. It is such an important area that mistakes can be extremely costly and very difficult to put right after the event.

Hairdressers are often loathe to use fringe benefits but, in fact, they are amongst the most attractive ways of recruiting and keeping staff. In Fig. 4.8 we suggest some benefits that may be appropriate for the hairdressing industry. Evidence shows that fringe benefits are good for attracting staff and offer a disincentive to leave.

The complexity of payment systems is immense but it is a motivational tool available to you and you should make as much use of it as possible to ensure that your business flourishes and grows.

### 4.3.4 Conclusions on motivation

We have seen motivating staff as involving a large number of elements which include:

- Staff must know what is expected of them and the implications of performance or non-performance.
- The owner or manager must understand what individually motivates their staff and try as far as possible to meet this where practical in the workplace.
- Regular meetings, systems and procedures for keeping staff involved and informed must be employed. This is to ensure that staff feel they have a role and purpose in working within their salon and that they can see where the business is heading and their part in helping to achieve the goals.
- The wage payment system must reward staff adequately for their needs in basic living terms and must be responsive to their efforts, performance and motivation and seen as fair and equally applied to all.

The above items are the building blocks for effective staff motivation; research, theory and practice will give us pointers to achieve these objectives within our own business.

## 4.4 Behaviour

### Managing problem people

In the previous sections on Communication and Motivation we gave some clues as to how to handle people. Most managers are brought up to believe that the answer to managing problem people is to do something to motivate them. The assumption is that people have to be prodded into action because, left to their own devices, they would do little or nothing. *Problem people rarely do nothing.* The problem usually arises because they are busy doing something other than what is required! The key to motivating people is to change the things that are preventing them from behaving as we would wish, rather than dream up all sorts of extra motivators. It is not that problem people are always demotivated – more probably, they are being motivated to do the wrong things.

There are two different approaches when it comes to managing people. One focuses on identifying and meeting people's needs and the other on managing people's behaviour.

The behaviour approach assumes that no behaviour occurs in a vacuum. Something always happens before it and something always happens after it. The surrounding events are crucial because they explain why the person is behaving as they are and give us ideas or clues as to how we can solve the problem. Things that happen before the behaviour in question are called 'triggers'. Things that happen after the behaviour are called 'reinforcers'.

While triggers and reinforcers remain intact and linked to the behaviour, it is predictable that the problem will continue. If either triggers or reinforcers, or both, are changed then it is inevitable that the behaviour will also change. The way to solve problems caused by other people's behaviour is therefore as follows:

| | |
|---|---|
| Step one | Be clear and specific about the problem behaviour. |
| Step two | Identify the events that trigger the behaviour. |
| Step three | Identify the reinforcers that are currently sustaining the problem behaviour. |
| Step four | Be clear and specific about what behaviour you want (usually the opposite to the behaviour you have got). |
| Step five | Work out how to change the triggers so that the problem behaviour is no longer triggered and the wanted behaviour is. |
| Step six | Work out how to change the reinforcers so that the problem behaviour is no longer encouraged and the wanted behaviour is. |
| Step seven | Check that your plan is feasible (that you really can put it into action and want to go through with it) and work out how to implement it. |
| Step eight | Finally, implement the changes and watch the problem behaviour decrease and the wanted behaviour increase. |

Eight steps might strike you as rather daunting but once you have used the 'behaviour approach' a few times, the formality of these steps can be relaxed and the whole approach seems more natural.

Initially, the most difficult part of the 'behaviour approach' is the novelty of concentrating solely on the external events that surround someone's behaviour. It seems more natural (because it is a more familiar way of thinking about people's behaviour) to slip into speculation about underlying motives, attitudes and feelings. The 'behaviour approach' doesn't deny the existence of such things. It merely recommends that for practical purposes you solve the problem by changing the external circumstances in which the behaviour occurs. It is your responsibility to manage problem people. Since your behaviour breeds their behaviour, you get the people you deserve.

*Keys to changing behaviour*

In the previous sections we have talked about managing people, communication and motivation and we would recommend further reading on this subject. Chapter 5 on discipline and handling staff problems will help to focus upon the key areas. To summarise, we suggest the following procedure:

- *The manager owns the problem*
  Tempting though it always is to blame the other person, the plain fact is that it is the manager's responsibility to do something to solve the problem. The manager always owns the problem.

- *The manager's behaviour breeds the subordinate's behaviour*
  In these cases we have seen how the manager unwittingly did things to create or aggravate the very problems they were suffering from. The manager's own behaviour is *always* a significant factor since the subordinate's behaviour is a reaction to it. It follows, therefore, that if the manager's behaviour changes, so will the subordinate's

- *The events surrounding behaviour always hold the key to changing it*
  The very essence of the 'behaviour approach' is to concentrate on what is happening before and after the behaviour in question. Triggers happen before and reinforcements after. Change the 'befores' and 'afters' and you change the behaviour.

- *The effectiveness of positive reinforcement must never be underestimated*
  Positive reinforcement has an important part to play in all the cases we have looked at. It is as simple as being careful to notice people, involve people, thank and congratulate people. The more often such reinforcers can happen after the desired behaviour, the more likely it is that the problem behaviour will decrease and the desired behaviour increase. Everyone likes positive reinforcement.

- *Modifying problem behaviour is a gradual process*
  Problem behaviours take a long time to establish themselves and it takes time to disestablish them and replace them with more desirable behaviours. The 'behaviour approach' is not magic. It depends for its success on breaking the links between triggers, problem behaviours and reinforcers. This is a gradual evolutionary process, like water dripping on a stone.

## 4.5 Leadership styles

Many of us in hairdressing have never considered the kind of style we adopt when managing staff and the potential advantages and disadvantages of each style. If we really wish to get the best from our staff we need to consider the range of possible leadership styles available to a manager. If we look at Fig. 4.9 we will see that 'boss' or 'control' centred leadership uses a high level of authority by the manager in stages 1 to 4 while in stages 4 to 7 there is an increasing area of freedom for subordinates in which to make decisions. The following is a closer look at each stage of the diagram.

**Fig. 4.9** Range of possible leadership behaviour.

*Stage one – the manager makes the decision and announces it*

In this case the boss or manager identifies a problem, considers alternative solutions, chooses one of them and reports his or her decision to the staff for action. He may or may not give consideration to what he believes his staff will think or feel about his decision. In most cases he will provide no opportunity for them to participate in the decision making process. Coercion may or may not be used or implied.

*Stage two – the manager 'sells' his decision*

In this particular management style the manager takes responsibility for identifying the problem and arriving at a decision. Rather than simply announcing it, however, he takes the additional step of 'selling' his subordinates the idea or persuading them to accept it. In doing so, he recognises the possibility of resistance by indicating what the benefits may be for the employees in carrying out the decision.

*Stage three – the manager presents his ideas and invites questions*

The manager may arrive at a decision and seek acceptance of the ideas by providing an opportunity for his staff to get a fuller explanation of his thinking and intentions. After presenting the idea, he invites questions so that his associates or staff can understand what he is trying to accomplish. This 'give and take' enables the manager and staff to explore more fully the implications of the decision.

*Stage four – the manager presents a tentative decision subject to change*

This kind of behaviour permits the subordintes to exert some influence on the decision. The initiative for identifying and diagnosing the problem, however, remains with the boss. Before the meeting with his staff, he may have thought the problem through and arrived at a decision even if it is only a tentative one. Before finalising it he proposes his solution for reaction. What he is really saying is, 'I would appreciate your reactions, but will reserve for myself the final decision.'

*Stage five – the manager presents the problem, gets suggestions then makes a decision*

Until this point the boss has come before the group with a solution of his own. At stage five the staff now get the chance to suggest solutions. The manager's initial role involves identifying the problem. He may say, 'We need to think of ideas to generate more new clients for the salon – what ideas do you have to help solve the problem?'

The function of the team or group becomes one of helping the manager to explore a wider range of solutions to the problem. The purpose is to capitalise on the knowledge and experience of those who are often at the sharp end. From this wider range of alternatives developed by the team, the manager then selects the solution that he regards as most appropriate or promising.

*Stage six – the manager defines the limits and requests the group to make a decision*

At this stage, the manager passes to the group or team the right to make decisions. Before doing so he may define the problem to be solved and the boundaries or guidelines within which the decision must be made. For example, he may state the budget limitations, the deadlines for completion or which particular staff must carry out some aspects of the decision.

*Stage seven – the manager permits the group to make the decision within prescribed limits*

This represents an extreme or total degree of group freedom only occasionally encountered in salon organisations. It is usually reserved for highly motivated staff, staff who have received a wide range of training or well educated staff who will not take kindly to decisions being imposed upon them, but feel they should be involved in accepting and taking responsibility for the problems and the solutions. Without their commitment the decision is unlikely to be implemented. Here the team undertakes the identification and diagnosis of the problem, develops alternative procedures for solving it and decides on one or more of the solutions. The only limits directly imposed on the group by the company are those specified by their manager. If the boss participates in the decision making process, he attempts to do so with no more authority than any other member of the group. He commits himself in advance to assist in implementing whatever decision the group makes.

*Conclusions*

In conclusion there are, of course, advantages and disadvantages in each leadership style. Leadership styles 1 to 4 tend to be implemented much more quickly as managers do not need to call meetings or involve the staff in the decision making process. The disadvantage is that when staff are not involved in the decision making process they may not be committed to carrying out the decision which will result in failure of action being carried out on a continual or on-going basis.

When staff are involved in the decision making process we are, in fact, introducing some of the motivational theories already expounded in the previous sections on managing people. Areas or items which directly affect the staff require them to be involved in the decision making process otherwise we may reap the reward of frustrated and demotivated staff and disruptive behaviour.

In conclusion, we must remember that if we have normally adopted management styles 1 to 4 where a high degree of authority of control was maintained by the manager we cannot suddenly expect the staff to solve problems and make decisions. Inconsistent behaviour by the manager will result in confusion and insecurity for the staff. If we wish to work towards a greater degree of freedom for our staff then we must gradually change our behaviour as managers over a period of time so that the staff become used to accepting responsibility and thinking through their ideas and proposals, particularly when they know that they may well be adopted into the business.

# Chapter Five
# Handling staff problems and disciplinary procedures

## 5.1 Discipline

Discipline involves two separate elements linked closely to ensure a reasonable and safe behaviour among staff so as to promote business success and to protect clients from injury or upset. The first is education and training to attempt to generate acceptance of and adherence to fair and reasonable rules and standards of work set by the organisation. The second is the procedure and response to be adopted when behaviour falls below these standards (the disciplinary procedure). This will also involve the punishments involved for repeated infringements.

In an ideal world we would have only self-discipline and there would never be any need for rules and procedures. But human nature being what it is, people need guidance and reminders as to what is expected of them, especially young or inexperienced staff. People often admit to having 'lazier selves' which if not checked get worse.

> 'I started being a few minutes late, then it was ten, then half an hour. Then I was told off. If they had said something at the beginning it would have been easier. Then you don't get into bad habits.'
>
> Interview with a Junior Stylist (London)

It is important not to see discipline as negative or punishment-centred. These attitudes are often symptoms of other staff problems and removal of the causes may make for better performance and improved profitability.

Staff are generally much happier when they know what is expected of them and the standards that they must meet as detailed in previous sections on managing people and job descriptions. They will gain security and confidence from knowing the boundaries within which they must act. This also protects them against victimisation and erratic treatment provided that the rules are fair and necessary.

An open approach to rules can be compared to police styles of traffic control. Which would you prefer?

(1) To receive a fine through the post for speeding measured by radar (unknown to you) and photographed licence plates
(2) Noticing a marked police car on the motorway and having to slow down to avoid being stopped

Which style of rules do you have in your salon? Which do you think your staff would prefer?

If you wish to ensure reasonable and safe behaviour amongst staff, the staff must know the following:

**Fig. 5.1** The disciplinary process.

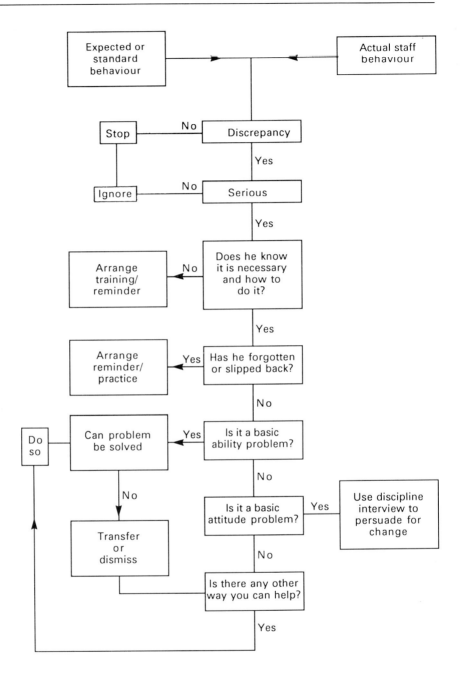

- What is expected of them and an indication of the standards as detailed in the sections on job descriptions (Chapter 3) and rules and regulations (below)
- What they are or are not allowed to do, and why
- What will happen if they fall below these standards or break the rules
- That these procedures will be applied equally and fairly to all staff for all infringements (not just the ones you do not like or the weakest ones)

Many salon managers and owners would ask the question, 'Why do I need to bother with all this?' We list below four reasons why all this is worthwhile:

(1) It promotes a better standard of work amongst staff and creates a better salon image.
(2) It increases morale and staff confidence and a positive attitude towards work.
(3) It reduces the amount of time spent in arguing the whys and wherefores of what is good and bad behaviour and encourages better working relationships.
(4) The salon will be better prepared for any complaints of unfair dismissal if you follow the guidelnes and introduce the documents recommended in this book.

Figure 5.1 illustrates in diagrammatical form the whole process of discipline. Note that a disciplinary interview or dismissing members of staff is the last resort, never the first. If we have gone to such pains to advertise, recruit, select and train staff it is short-sighted to dismiss staff because we are, as management, unable to handle the situation.

If we wish to handle staff problems and to ensure that standards and codes of behaviour are fairly applied to all members of staff then we must introduce written rules and regulations so that staff know what is expected of them.

## 5.2 Procedure for producing rules

Rules may cover a wide range of activities but we provide a checklist of possible areas that rules may need to cover in salons (see Fig. 5.2). You may or may not wish to include all of these in your own set of rules.

It is essential to have a *clear reason* behind the rules and to explain why all these rules are necessary. Nothing causes more hostility than a bad or unfair rule or one which is clearly old-fashioned or stupid. Resentment can be avoided if adequate explanations are given and rules are based on logic and reason. Rules based on prejudice or emotion will simply encourage 'rule breaking' and 'beating the system'.

### Standards of job performance

In addition to rules, staff need to know what standards are required of them and how these will be measured. The basic document for this is the job description. This has been explained in some detail in Chapter 3 which also gives some examples of specimen job descriptions for hairdressing jobs. The job descriptions supplied are an outline so that readers can identify the key areas in defining the job.

**Fig. 5.2** Areas
for rules to cover
in salons.

(1) Protection of company facilities/safety
   - Security
   - Handling of money and valuables
   - Treatment of equipment, furniture etc
   - Smoking
   - Weapons
   - Handling hazardous chemicals etc.
   - What to do in case of fire, bomb threat or holdups (robbery) or other emergency
   - Health, hygiene and Safety Regulations

(2) Respect for company property
   - Damaging or defacing property
   - Use of company time
   - Use of company resources (telephone, equipment, lotions etc.)
   - Personal calls
   - Valuables etc.
   - Works areas etc., tidiness
   - Uniforms and dress

(3) Completing company records (accuracy and truthfulness)
   - Bookings
   - Timesheets
   - Expense claims

(4) Punctuality, absence, sickness, attendance
   - Procedure to be followed
   - Approval in advance
   - Standards required

(5) Use of alcohol or drugs

(6) Gambling or other activities

(7) Respect for other staff/clients
   - Distributing unauthorised material
   - Abusive language, fights, arguments
   - Eating, chewing, sexual harassment etc.
   - Obeying senior staff
   - Infectious diseases

(8) Confidentiality
   - Documents of business
   - Information about business
   - Surveys (taking part)
   - Financial performance

(9) Care and maintenance of stock

(10) Vigilance over theft
   - What to do if you see this happening

**Sample misconduct and disciplinary rules/procedure**
The Company reserves the right to terminate employment in cases of misconduct or failure to comply with the Company's regulations, or when artistically or technically the employee does not reach or maintain the standard required by the Company in accordance with their job description. The Company's disciplinary rules are contained in this Company Manual.

(1) The employee will not normally be dismissed for a first offence, except in cases of gross misconduct. Gross misconduct is:

- Where an employee's work involves accounting for or handling cash and fails to comply with instructions as laid down by the Company.
- Drunkenness which would seriously endanger the salon, staff or clients.
- Items of equipment or stock belonging to the Company removed from the premises at any time, either intentionally or unintentionally.
- An employee approaches, solicits or accepts custom from any person who is a customer of any salon within the Company and undertakes services for them outside the premises.
- Any serious offence which has been finally warned to the employee previously.

(2) The following procedure will take place unless for cases of gross misconduct:

- Verbal warning by immediate superior, i.e. manager, in the *presence of a third person* and a file note forwarded to the administrator for record purposes.
- Second verbal warning, procedure as above, but the subject of the second warning *must be the same subject* as the first warning.
- Third and final warning resulting in possible dismissal. Details to be communicated to the managing director. Third and final warnings will only be carried out by the managing director. They *must* be put in writing to the employee stating the reason for the warning, the dates of the previous warnings and the time limit set before the warning is reviewed. Final warnings must be on the same subject as the two previous warnings, i.e. the three warnings cannot be given on time-keeping for first warning, technical ability for second warning.
  Accurate records of what was said, the date of the conversation, who was present and the time limit set before the next review must be forwarded to the administrator for safe keeping.

(3) The policy is such that disciplinary action will be taken only when:

- There is good and clear evidence of some offence.
- It will be demonstrably fair and consistent with the offence committed.
- A member of staff can be represented.
- Staff have a right of appeal (see below)

(4) All staff will have access to a set of up to date rules and regulations of the company.

(5) There is a right of appeal for any member of staff to the Directors of the Company. Appeals must be notified within 48 hours of disciplinary action. Management reserves the right to hold a disciplinary hearing when all interested parties will be invited to attend.

(6)  The results of any disciplinary action will be held on file for no more than two years after the offence.

If in doubt on disciplinary procedures always check before speaking to the employee *not afterwards*.

## 5.3 The disciplinary process

Once a salon has the following two documents it becomes much easier to measure and identify if staff do not meet the standard expected:

- written rules and regulations
- job descriptions

You may now need to apply some kind of disciplinary procedure. Not every kind of organisation needs disciplinary procedures but the advantage of a written code resolves ambiguity and introduces good management practice.
  A disciplinary procedure should include all of the following features:

(1)  Provision for both informal and formal warnings before disciplinary action is taken
(2)  An indication of the range of disciplinary actions that may be taken
(3)  A reference to any set of rules or standards which will form the basis of any decision to discipline, including those items of 'gross misconduct' rendering the employee liable to summary dismissal
(4)  Any appeals procedure against the result of a disciplinary enquiry

**Fig. 5.3**
Guidelines on disciplinary procedures contained in the Code of Practice (20 June 1977 issue).

Disciplinary procedure should:

(1)  Be in writing.
(2)  Specify to whom it applies.
(3)  Provide for matters to be dealt with quickly.
(4)  Indicate the disciplinary actions which may be taken.
(5)  Specify the levels of management which have the authority to take the various forms of disciplinary action, ensuring that immediate superiors do not normally have the power to dismiss without reference to senior management.
(6)  Provide for individuals to be informed of the complaints against them and to be given the opportunity to state their case before decisions are reached.
(7)  Give individuals the right to be accompanied by a trade union representative or by a fellow employee of their choice.
(8)  Ensure that, except for gross misconduct, no employees are dismissed for a first breach of discipline.
(9)  Ensure that disciplinary action is not taken until the case has been carefully investigated.
(10)  *Ensure that individuals are given an explanation for any penalty imposed.*
(11)  Provide a right of appeal and specify the procedure to be followed.

(ACAS published by DOE (HMSO): obtainable from local office)

(5) Indications of any written records kept about an employee and the length of time held before removal from the employee's file, e.g. absenteeism and lateness records

A sample disciplinary procedure is listed in Fig. 5.3. It is also advisable to check that:

(1) The disciplinary procedure does not conflict with the ACAS Code of Practice
(2) Staff have personal access to copies of rules and regulations, job descriptions and disciplinary procedures
(3) Disciplinary procedures do not apply where problems arise due to staff incapability rather than culpability
(4) All staff responsible for carrying out disciplinary procedures are aware of the ACAS Code of Practice

## 5.4 The disciplinary interview

The disciplinary interview is a problem solving interview whose aims are to:

- Establish facts and determine who is to blame
- Weigh up both sides of the issue
- Formulate action plans to try to achieve results and eliminate the problem

The purpose of a disciplinary interview lies in letting people know where they are falling short of the standards expected and of any breaches of rules. It also serves as a means of identifying other problems in the company which may emerge at the interview. It is for this reason that we must be aware of and understand the various communication techniques detailed in Chapter 4 and, in particular, the barriers to active listening. One of the greatest mistakes that managers make at disciplinary interviews is spending far too much time talking and not enough time listening. From an employee's point of view there is nothing worse than sentence being passed before all the evidence has emerged at the interview. The main stages of a disciplinary interview are shown in Fig. 5.4.

There are a number of approaches that an interviewer can take to a disciplinary interview:

(1) conspiritorial
(2) stress
(3) tell and sell
(4) tell and listen
(5) joint problem solving

Professional interviewers would recommend (5) as the most realistic approach to disciplinary interviewing. Figure 5.5 compares these approaches and notes the pros and cons of each. A number of physical items need to be borne in mind when interviewing and we list these below:

(1) Avoid extremes of heat and cold and ensure adequate ventilation,
(2) Avoid extremes of light and dark, e.g. lights shining into eyes.
(3) Ensure that conditions of privacy exist – not in a corridor or public room.
(4) Eliminate interruptions, e.q. phone calls and other staff.
(5) Choose chairs which are reasonably comfortable and easy to sit in.
(6) Set things up so that you are facing one another.

(7)  Provide water and an ashtray if appropriate.
(8)  Ensure you have the interviewee's job description and all other relevant documents available.

## 5.5  Conclusions

In conclusion, therefore the principles for effective discipline are:

- Discipline as close to the offence as possible.
- Ensure there is a clear set of rules or standards and the staff know what these are.
- Never discipline in public, always in private.
- Do not have favourites – nothing undermines discipline faster.
- Discipline in a *calm and neutral frame of mind*. Shouting, yelling, swearing, throwing things, sarcasm and insults contribute nothing and are counter productive, leading to mistakes and apologies.
- The aim of discipline is primarily to correct behaviour and only in the last resort to punish when training or counselling have not been effective.
- Concentrate when disciplining on things which can be changed by the employee, not personal characteristics. We can never change a personality, therefore we must concentrate on the problem.
- Be fair, firm and *consistent*. Rules require monitoring and disciplining for every breach but ensure that the 'punishments' are suited to the 'crimes'.

**Fig. 5.4**
Disciplinary
interview – main
stages.

Preparation before the interview
(1)  Ensure the interviewee knows the purpose.
(2)  Collect as much evidence as possible before the interview e.g. job description/standards/rules and regulations/procedure etc.
(3)  Examine employee's past record/performance.
(4)  Determine your personal strategy (see text).

The interview itself
(1)  Explain the purpose of the interview.

(2)  Establish the facts as far as possible.
  - No evidence – no case.
  - Ask employee for his version/explanation.
  - Hear witnesses (if relevant).
  - Go over key points until you are clear.
  - Adjourn if insufficient information.

(3)  Agree facts with interviewee.
  - Establish areas of agreement.
  - Explain reasons for required changes.

(4)  Establish responsibilities.
  - Examine reasons for problems.
  - Examine special or mitigating circumstances.

(5)  Agree future course of action.
  - Agree standards and changes to close difference.
  - Agree any support/help to be given.
  - Agree any sanctions/penalties applicable.
  - Agree review date for improvement.

| Strategy | Description/example | Advantages (pros) | Disadvantages (cons) |
|---|---|---|---|
| (1) Conspiratorial approach | Conspiring with interviewee against the system. e.g. Let's solve this together in spite of them. | Helps reluctant interviewee to talk. Removes guilt from interviewer who hates doing it. | Can be easily misunderstood and cause future problems. Punishment necessary. Perverts the real objective of interview. |
| (2) Stress approach | Give interviewee a 'hard time'. e.g. You may as well confess – we know what you have been doing. | Interviewer feels powerful. Interviewee may confess and promise to improve. Young females find this difficult to take. | No real evidence of any real commitment to change. May disillusion staff. Encourages aggression, lying, dishonesty as defence. |
| (3) Tell and sell | Explain situation and consequences and reasons behind it and persuade employee to improve. e.g. If you could just remember to clock in/ out properly each time . . . | Useful for young people who may not link actions to their consequences. Also compensates for where staff are unclear about rules, procedures and punishments. | Requires persuasive skills on part of interviewer. Some rules may be difficult to sell to staff. |
| (4) Tell and listen | Explain as in (3) above then listen to interviewee's explanations weighing up consequences. Useful in clarifying areas of uncertainty. Usually leads into (5). | Wide application where manager wishes to stay friendly and acquaint staff with facts. Needs to be rounded off by agreeing course of action. | Many managers are all tell and no listen (as in (3)). Some staff may be over-zealous and not listen to you! |
| (5) Joint problem solving | Encourage staff to identify for themselves with your help what has gone wrong and what should be done. Requires a flexible approach to staff problems. | Useful for preventing staff becoming 'case-hardened' and habitual offenders. Often works where all other methods have failed. | Takes longer. Requires most skill and sensitivity to staff. Skill in open questions and listening absolutely essential. |

**Fig. 5.5** Disciplinary interviewing strategies.

- Follow a set of guidelines for disciplinary action as shown in Fig. 5.4.
- Do not carry private discipline into the open with snide references. When you have completed the interview, you should get back onto normal terms with the staff as soon as possible and not harbour grudges.

If you follow the above procedures then you will ensure that you do not have to:

- Reverse decisions
- Cope with increased staff resentment
- Lose tribunals or other legal actions, a strong motivator to ensure you get procedure correct

We can all improve and can find time to do so if we want. Many salon owners do so constantly but others all too frequently wait for events to happen to them. The barrier to improvement is always apathy, arrogance, and priorities placed elsewhere.

# Chapter Six
# Training

## 6.1 Introduction

Training is a systematic development of the knowledge, skills and attitudes required by an individual to perform adequately a given task or job. Training involves learning of various kinds and in various situations. Learning may be something that the trainee wants to do for him or herself, or it may be necessary to provide it for that person. If training is provided or offered, the individual may need to be given an incentive – in other words to be motivated – to learn and to apply the learning. Even if the trainee is self-motivated it may still be necessary to provide guidance and training which will help the person to channel or focus his/her enthusiasm towards a worthwhile goal.

Training can take place in a number of ways – on the job or off the job, in the company or outside the company. It can involve the use of many techniques such as:

- Demonstrations
- Practice
- Coaching
- Guided reading
- Lectures
- Talks
- Discussions
- Case studies
- Role playing
- Assignments
- Projects
- Group exercises
- Programmed learning
- The discovery method

These techniques can be provided by a wide range of people such as:

- Specialist company trainers
- Managers
- Supervisors
- Colleagues/stylists
- External trainers
- Educationalists

The step-by-step process towards training is as follows:

(1) Identification and analysis of training needs
(2) Defining the objectives
(3) Preparation of training plans and programmes
(4) Implementation of the plans
(5) Measuring and analysing the results
(6) Evaluation of training programmes and techniques

## 6.2 Identification and analysis of training needs

The analysis of training needs aims to define the gap or difference between what is actually happening now and what should, or is expected to, happen in the future. Training needs should be analysed into three areas:

*(1)  The company or the salon as a whole*

To analyse the company or the salon as a whole defining the salon's strengths and weaknesses and the salon or company's future requirements. For example the salon may be operating in a changing environment whereby more competitors are opening in the town or city. This may require the salon to adopt a different approach towards the services it offers, the pricing strategy of the salon and the range of work that the stylists may be expected to achieve. Computerisation on reception for client records may be an area where the company needs to develop its skills to offer a comprehensive service or to personalise promotional methods.

*(2)  Individual salons*

The salon as part of a group may lack certain expertise or skills, for example the salon group as a whole may have a good knowledge of hairdressing, colouring or perming skills but an individual salon may be weak in one of these areas.

*(3)  Individuals*

Certain staff within the organisation will need to be trained to develop their potential. They may be grouped together with a common training need, e.g. training in long hair work or mens hairdressing, or they may need to receive individual training.

*Methods of analysis*

There are three basic methods of analysing training needs:

(1)  *Surveys*
   - Client satisfaction survey
   - Staff questionnaires
   - Competitors' analysis
   - Market street surveys
   (See Chapter 1 on Marketing and promotions for further information regarding the examples given.)
(2)  *Job analysis*
   - A broad analysis of the needs of the job and any special problems which may be seen by the job holder, his/her manager and possibly colleagues
   - A detailed study of the responsibiities, duties and tasks carried out which forms the basis for a job description
   - An analysis of the knowledge and skills required by the job holder which forms the basis of a job description
   - A description of the training requirements to meet the needs of the job
   (See Chapter 3, Section 3.2 Analysing the job.)
(3)  *Performance/assessment appraisal*
   - Assesses the performance of individuals against agreed objectives and standards already set and clearly defined within the organisation and will consider potential for promotion

- Establishes the gaps in knowledge, weaknesses in doing the job and areas to be developed if the individual is to progress

(See Chapter 3, Section 3.11 Integration of new staff. See also the Appendix Sources of further information for further reading on staff appraisal.)

## 6.3 Defining the objectives

Training must aim to achieve *measurable goals* expressed in terms of improved performance by individuals, a salon as part of a group, or a company as a whole. The goals must be realistic and achievable and you need to remember that you cannot train people to change their personalities, you can only develop them by various training techniques to learn skills and to want to apply them.

As explained in Chapter 3, job descriptions must have clearly defined areas of responsibility and levels of authority with minimum standards which are measurable and achievable. Training objectives, like job descriptions, which are vague and woolly will result in the training being difficult to measure. The reason why many owners and managers of salons are not committed to training is often because the aims and objectives were not clearly defined in the first place.

Sending staff upon training courses without individuals knowing why they are attending or what they are hoping to achieve or, even worse, being sent on a training programme as a punishment to 'get their act together' tends to have a demotivating effect.

*Implications of training*

There are many long term benefits of training but it would be foolish to pretend there are no disadvantages. These disadvantages occur when owners or managers (or training experts!) have not clearly identified the real training needs. Detailed below are potential problem areas which may occur:

| Cause | Effect |
|---|---|
| Staff sent on course as appeasement but not allowed to put into practice new skills and/or behaviour. | Frustration, demotivation, deterioration in performance. |
| No clearly defined responsibilities. | Frustration, demotivation, deterioration in performance and/or behaviour. |
| No clearly defined authority. | Frustration, demotivation, deterioration in performance and/or behaviour. |
| No involvement in decision making. | Frustration, demotivation, deterioration in performance and/or behaviour. |
| Disruptive behaviour. | Deterioration in performance and/or behaviour, staff leaving. |

| | |
|---|---|
| No consultation on decisions that directly affect the staff. | Frustration, demotivation, failure to contribute ideas in the future, staff leaving. |
| Authoritarian management style. | Frustration, demotivation, staff resignation. |
| Increased confidence by learning new skills. | Challenging decisions and superiors, questioning policy, potential resignation if staff not listened to. |
| Third party reinforcement of own views. | Challenging decisions and superiors, questioning policy, potential resignation if no change in operation of business. |

Read Chapter 3, Section 3.2 Analysing the job and Chapter 4 Managing people for further understanding on why these problems may occur.

## 6.4 Planning the programme

Training programmes should be based on the analysis of training needs and should include:

(1) A definition of the objectives, describing the outcome of training in terms of the results or behaviour expected. In other words, what the trainee will be doing after having achieved the objective, e.g.:

At the end of a training course in selling retail products the stylist will be able to sell a range of retail products to 10 per cent of all clients visiting the salon.

(2) Details of:

  • Timing/length of programme (days of the week and times during the day)
  • Content of the programme – subject headings
  • Methods of training – lectures, role playing, project work
  • Who will train
  • Venue or place of training – on/off the job, in or outside the company

(3) The method by which the training will be evaluated – one-to-one interviews, surveys.
(4) Estimate of costs.

*Timing/length of programme*

When planning the timing and length of the programme take into consideration the following factors:

  • Operational needs, e.g. salon opening hours
  • Individual's age and experience
  • Barriers to learning, e.g. tiredness at end of the day, noise, interruptions

(See section 4.2 Communication.)

*Contents of programme*

Plan the programme to take into account the following points:

(1) Logical structure. Define the programme into a logical structure with key subject headings.
(2) Context. Start by explaining the whole story or the whole picture. What is the objective or the goal of the training programme and where does it fit into the whole plan or story of their job or the salon or organisation in which they work?
(3) Explain why the job has to be done.
(4) Never just teach a process.
(5) Then teach the detailed process the trainee must learn to achieve the goal.

*Digestible chunks*

Present the information or training programme in amounts that the trainee can cope with. Read Section 4.2 Communication, particularly on the process of communication, questioning techniques and active listening.

*Know your trainees*

Adjust your approach to meet the needs and ability of the trainee, e.g. hairdressing trainees, senior stylists, managers.

*Link the training to the trainee's existing knowledge*

Draw on the previous experience of the trainee and link this to the job to be learnt. Give illustrations and examples wherever possible.

*Concentrate on positive instructions*

Avoid negative instruction; talk about and demonstrate the right way to approach a job.

*Give the trainee feedback on progress*

Tell the trainee how they are doing and give praise and encouragement.

*Allow the trainee time to practise*

Practice reinforces understanding and learning.

### 6.4.1 Training techniques

The main training techniques available can be divided into three areas:

(1) On the job techniques.
(2) On or off the job techniques.
(3) Off the job techniques.

*On the job techniques*

*Demonstrations* This requires telling or showing a trainee how to do a job and then allowing them to get on with it. This is the most common and effective method as long as it is done properly, i.e. by a trained instructor following a logical training programme based on job analysis and the practical application of it. It is also essential that the instructor has received training in training techniques and preferably undergone a professional training course such as City and Guilds Certificate in Hairdressing Management (NCVQ Level 4), has good communication skills and understands the psychological aspects of training.

*Coaching* In which counselling takes place, usually between the manager and staff and preferably based upon performance and/or assessment/ appraisal.

*Job rotation* This method broadens staff experience by moving them from job to job. Many hairdressing trainees rotate on a regular three monthly basis to work with individual stylists whereby they can learn from each individual's techniques. This is an effective way as long as the learning experience is properly planned and controlled and that staff to whom they have been allocated have competent skills.

*On or off the job techniques*

*Job instruction* This occurs when there is a sequence of:

- Preparation
- Presentation, usually involving an explanation and demonstration of the skill
- Practice of the skill
- Testing of the new skill
- Follow-up or evaluation of subject or skill learnt, e.g. hairdressing demonstration then the opportunity to practise and be evaluated

*Assignments or projects* When trainees are asked to complete tasks or investigations with the aim of improving their knowledge of a particular subject and of developing skills in seeking and analysing information, creating new ideas and presenting results, e.g. hair product knowledge training whereby trainees learn the products, their features and benefits, use the products until they feel confident with them, produce suggestions or ideas as to how they would apply the products and present their findings to the rest of the group.

*Off the job techniques*

*Lectures/seminars* Talks designed to transfer information to an audience using controlled content and timings. Lectures may appear to be the best way of increasing knowledge but they are limited by the capacity of the individuals to absorb what has been heard – which could be as little as 20 per cent. This can be caused by the size of the audience, the language and speed at which the lecturer delivers the material, the complexity or lack of visual aids or environmental barriers such as noise and interruptions.

In the author's experience, this is the least effective of training techniques as the audience often pick up and absorb what they want to hear without understanding how they may apply the information unless other training techniques are used to reinforce the objective.

*Discussion* Discussion techniques which aim to get a group to participate actively in learning and to give people a chance to learn from the experience of others.

*Discovery method* This style of instruction allows the trainee to learn by finding out principles of a subject for him/herself but must be backed up with suitable guidance from the instructor.

*Programmed learning/open learning* A text which progressively feeds information to trainees, e.g. open learning, correspondence course. After each piece of information is delivered or given, questions are asked either verbally or through a computer or reading material which the trainee should answer correctly before moving on. There are now some hairdressing open learning videos and ISM produce a *Salon Management Fax Guide* which uses this technique.

*Case studies* These are descriptions of an event or situation which the trainees analyse in order to diagnose the cause of the problem and work out how to solve it.

*Role playing* Where participants practise skills by acting out a situation, assuming the roles of the characters, e.g. recruitment/selection techniques, disciplinary interviewing techniques, counselling techniques, assessment/appraisal.

*Group exercises* In which trainees examine problems and work out solutions as a group, e.g. creative brain storming, group project work.

### 6.4.2 Aids to training

*Visual aids*

Visual aids have three main uses:

(1) To convey information
(2) To reinforce the spoken word
(3) To provide background information and atmosphere

*To convey information* They should be used whenever information can be conveyed more effectively by visual means especially:

- to give a breakdown or analysis of complicated information
- to show the stages in a process
- to provide evidence and examples of people, places or objects to support the discussion or presentation

Visual aids such as films or video tapes are the most interesting, but should not be allowed to play for too long as they can detract from the talk.

*To reinforce the spoken word* Visual and audio/visual aids can be used to introduce a spoken text, to link one part of a presentation to another, to summarise a sequence of ideas or pose or ask a question.

*To provide background information and atmosphere* Static visual aids such as photographs of a new company logo, posters, charts, product packs, can be set up beforehand and left throughout the presentation. They can provide an alternative subject of focus to the speaker, something else which the audience can look at to reinforce the theme.

Visual and audio aids can also help set the tone and mood of the presentation. The choice should depend not only on the subject, but on the venue as well as the size and nature of the audience, e.g. young hairdressers would require a different stimulus from a presentation than a 'long in the tooth' company of sales representatives!

*General guidelines for visual aids*

- Projected visuals, e.g. films, slides, OHPs, are easy to see because they are magnified.
- Too many types of visual aids in one presentation may be difficult to co-ordinate and may actually distract the audience.
- Never use existing visual material just because it happens to be available, e.g. an out-of-date photograph or poster. Making-do will probably hinder rather than help you reach your objectives.
- Order all materials at the earliest possible date. They often take time to prepare and should be available in time for checking and rehearsal.
- Make sure all the necessary equipment will be available at the rehearsal or training session, e.g. spare bulbs, leads, plug adapters.
- Keep a list of all the visual aids you plan to use and make a note of them in your training programme or script to jog your memory.
- If creating visual material during your training session, e.g. writing on flip charts or acetates, always remember the following:

  Have an outline of figures or notes pre-planned (so you are not left counting on your fingers!)
  Check the quality of the pens for the overhead projector or flip chart (keep the caps on until you need them). Only use this method if your printing is legible and you know how to spell any difficult words.
  Wherever possible use a flip chart or board you can stand beside *not one on the wall behind you.*

*Audience capacity of visual aids*

Remember the following statistics:

- Flip chart messages can be seen by 15 people and no more.
- OHP transparencies will reach up to 50 viewers if you have a long 'throw' from machine to screen.
- Video cassette/TV will reach up to 20 people per 24 inch screen. Good quality, big screen video projection will reach up to 100 people.
- 35 mm slides can be magnified to reach 100 people.

*How to use visual aids*

Remember the '4 Ps':

(1) Plan
(2) Presentation

(3) Precaution
(4) Performance

*Plan*
- Don't use unnecessary slides.
- Make sure all the information you need is available.
- Use slides for impact when words would confuse the audience. We all listen at the same speed but read at different speeds.
- Introduce colour. Colour has more impact than black and white.
- Use large writing and very few words. The more information on the slide, the less impact it will have.
- Make sure that you use words on the slide to emphasise the main point.
- Make sure the diagrams are readable.

*Presentation*
- Check all the equipment and paperwork is available and in good running order.
- Check that the slides, films or diagrams are the right way up.
- Check that the visual aids are in focus.
- Check that the slides or diagrams are in sequential order.
- Check the room for electrical sockets, acoustics, window closing and blinds, visibility of the audience.
- Never make last minute major alterations in the presentation as this will confuse you and the audience.

*Precautions*
- If more than one person is taking part it is essential that a full rehearsal is carried out. Always expect the worst to happen and be prepared for it.

*Performance*
- Do not ignore the diagrams and slides.
- Do not stand between the audience and the screen so that they cannot see.
- Do not keep looking over your shoulder at every slide change.
- Do not talk to the screen.
- Do not hold the slide for too long – if you leave it on the screen it will detract from what you are saying.

*Hints on preparing a notes system*

Unless you are a very experienced speaker or trainer do not rely upon your visual aids as your only notes – what happens if the equipment doesn't work?
Bearing in mind that many people have difficulty in spelling it is essential to prepare a notes system and to familiarise yourself with the spelling of certain words. Use the following guidelines:

(1) Always prepare your notes or script yourself. Only you know how the information should flow and which parts should be set out with special emphasis.
(2) Avoid flimsy paper for scripts – cards are easier to hold. Write on one side only and number each one clearly in the top right hand corner.
(3) Do not staple sheets or cards together; put to one side each card when you have completed delivery of it.
(4) Use different colours to mark the places where you intend to use visual aids or invite audience participation.

(5) Attach photocopies of any transparencies to the appropriate notes.
(6) If you have difficulty with spelling use the following ideas when writing on a flip chart:

- Get a member of the audience to write for you so you can concentrate on the feedback
- Get the feedback and have a pre-planned list already written out
- Have a card system of common words which tend to be used in your training sessions

We have tended to concentrate upon visual aids used in a training session such as videos, films, slides and OHP transparencies but there are alternative methods of reinforcing training such as:

- Audio cassette tapes which can be used to reinforce the learning message at a later date when the trainee is on his/her own
- Diagrams as part of handouts
- Books for additional in-depth reading and to be absorbed at the trainee's own pace
- Games which can introduce the fun element to learning
- Competitions/quizzes which introduce the discovery method but in an amusing way

*Venue or place of training*

Check all the physical and environmental arrangements:

(1) Is there sufficient seating and is it comfortable to sit for long periods of time?
(2) Can everyone see and hear?
(3) Can interruptions be avoided including the telephone?
(4) Ensure the temperature is not too hot or too cold.
(5) Ensure the environment is quiet.
(6) Provide ashtrays for smokers and segregate non-smokers if they wish. Alternatively, ban smoking but have a 'smoke break'.

*Estimate of costs*

Many enthusiastic trainers forget that the first question a salon owner or manager will ask: 'How much?' The costs need to cover the following:

- Development of training programme
- Training aids, e.g. films, equipment, production of training handouts
- Cost of venue and refreshments
- Lost revenue

Training is always a long term investment but business owners and managers tend to focus on the short term lost revenue as opposed to the long term benefits of developing people. The hairdressing industry is no exception to this attitude. Many salon owners view training as negative on the basis that 'if I train them they will leave and become my competitors' but the question to pose is, 'Can I afford not to train?' Within the industry the most valuable resource available to make businesses grow and prosper is people. If we build our people, our people will build our business – without people we might as well become self-employed mobile hairdressers with hairdressing salons becoming a thing of the past.

## 6.5 Evaluating the training

Training is evaluated by comparing its objectives or goals with its effects or outcome to discover how far it has achieved its purpose. Evaluation can take place at a number of levels:

- *Reactions* The immediate reaction of trainees to the training – how useful they feel it is, what they think of individual sessions and speakers, what they would like to put in or take out.
- *Learning* The measurement of the skills or knowledge trainees have gained as a result of training, e.g. a greater understanding of communication techniques, a heightened awareness of how speed in technical training methods can increase overall profitability to the salon.
- *Job behaviour* The assessment of how trainees have applied their training on the job.
- *Impact* The extent to which the behaviour of trainees, after training, has improved the performance of the 'individual, the salon and the whole organisation, e.g. after retail sales training has the retail sales percentage increased?

*Methods of evaluation*

- Comparison of targets prior to and after training
- Comparison of job performance to job description
- One to one interviews
- Surveys (dependent upon the training received)
- Behaviour of staff who have attended training

*Evaluation of the trainer*

At the end of each training session all good trainers should be prepared to ask the following questions:

(1) Did I prepare well?
(2) Did I put the job into context?
(3) Did I advise the learner what to expect in terms of both the job and the training time involved?
(4) Did I break the job down into digestible chunks?
(5) Did I put the training over in the right sequence?
(6) Did I bring out the key points?
(7) Did I show confidence and enthusiasm?
(8) Did I get and maintain the learner's interest?
(9) Did I get the learner to participate?
(10) Did I ask the right questions?
(11) Did I make proper use of the equipment and material for demonstration and practice?
(12) Did I use my notes?
(13) Did I follow through my instructions to evaluate effectiveness?
(14) Did the learner know how he/she was getting on?
(15) Did I ensure the learner's final performance was up to standard?

# Chapter Seven
# Planning and organisation

There are many reasons why clients visit a hairdresser – the majority of them are nothing to do with having their hair cut! This is covered in detail in the sections on promotions (Chapter 1) and motivation (Chapter 4). Equally important is the effect that bad planning and organisation have upon productivity which, in turn, affects the potential turnover and profitability of the business.

Planning can be categorised into the following key areas:

(1) Planning the salon
(2) Planning the work
(3) Planning your time
(4) Planning your staff's time

Points (1) and (2) are discussed in this chapter and points (3) and (4) in Chapter 8.

## 7.1 Planning the salon

Planning the salon layout is a key element in achieving a successful, profitable salon where the staff and clients enjoy the hairdressing experience. Salon owners often spend a substantial amount of time selecting the decor and image of a new salon as a kind of extension of their own personality but too little attention is paid to the work flow aspect and the effect it has upon:

- Client comfort
- Staff comfort and efficiency
- Productivity levels
- Marketing
- Meeting legislation requirements, e.g. Health and Safety at Work Act (see Chapter 9)

### 7.1.1 Client comfort

Clients perceive part of the image of the salon by its efficiency and comfort. This will affect whether they return to the salon because it has been an enjoyable experience and/or whether they will recommend it to their friends.

We need to consider the following points when planning a new salon:

- Access to reception
- Security of coats and belongings
- Comfortable seating in reception
- Comfortable seating at the backwash
- Comfortable seating at the styling position
- Access to backwashes and styling positions

- Heating and ventilation
- Lighting
- Access to toilets
- Conditions of toilet facilities
- Colour scheme

## 7.1.2 Staff comfort and efficiency

Staff will be more productive, particularly on busy days, if we consider the following points when planning a salon:

- Heating and ventilation
- Lighting
- Floor surfaces – easy to walk on, easy to clean
- Work surfaces – easy to clean, no sharp or dangerous edges
- Access to stock cupboard
- Access to dispensary
- Distance from backwash to styling position
- Access to coat and gown cupboard
- Access/distance to refreshment making facilities
- Optimum space for styling position
- Uncluttered traffic flow areas
- Colour schemes and their effect on the eye and psyche

## 7.1.3 Productivity levels

*Reception area*

When planning the layout of the salon how much thought is given to the size and space of the reception area? Is it too small making it difficult for staff to perform their jobs efficiently? Does it take up more than 15–20 per cent of the salon area? How much lost productivity area has been used by the reception desk? We must ask the question, 'Why do we have a reception area at all?'

The purpose of a reception area is to:

(1)  Project the initial image of the salon
(2)  Welcome clients and put them at ease
(3)  Provide facilities for clients to enter and depart with ease (particularly on busy days)
(4)  Provide facilities to house coats and gowns
(5)  Provide waiting facilities
(6)  Provide a consultaton area (optional)

How many salons meet all the above criteria?

*Backwash/styling positions*

From frequent visits to hairdressing salons we have come to the conclusion that backwash chairs were designed by men! Otherwise, why is there no allowance made for the fact that female clients are often between 5'3" and 5'6"in height and that we are not physically structured to have a straight shape from knee to shoulder! The shortcomings of chairs and backwashes are emphasised further when undergoing perming or colouring processes.

Why are backwashes positioned some distance from the styling position so that staff walk several miles each day between the two key areas in the salon? Even worse if they are up or down a number of steps. How much time is lost in productivity by the inefficient placement of key areas?

How much thought is given to easy access of equipment, e.g. trolleys, dispensary, electrical points and sterilisers, and the productivity time lost in reaching and using them?

Does the salon have adjustable styling chairs? Think of productivity loss due to absenteeism when staff are absent with bad backs or slipped discs when adjustable chairs would have solved the problem!

*Refreshments*

When offering clients refreshments, have the facilities available to supply them been considered? How long does it take to walk up a flight of stairs, wait for a kettle to boil and return with the drink? Has the time been costed into the pricing structure? Are there other ways of reducing the time element such as a thermostatic hot water boiler, a dish washer and a duty rota for staff to ensure that everyone helps keep the refreshment making area clean?

The average time to make a drink, including washing the cup and saucer, will be 6–10 minutes. Calculate how many clients have refreshments over a week and then a year! Think of the lost productivity time usually because this element of the service was not planned in the first place.

The answer to the planning and organisation of the salon layout is to adopt what is known as 'helicopter vision' and look at the traffic flow and stress points or to sit at key areas in the salon so that alternative ways of working can be achieved even in the smallest of spaces.

## 7.2 Planning the work

When planning work within the salon we often simply respond to the clients' wishes but, with a little forethought, we could ensure that the work flows easily and smoothly throughout the day instead of in the usual stop/go pattern.

### 7.2.1 Appointment systems

The majority of impulse visits to salons occur late morning or during the afternoon, very rarely at the beginning of the day. If we wish to maximise productivity we must fill up the appointment book systematically wherever possible. This involves booking clients into the salon by offering them the 'either/or' technique.

*Example*
Receptionist: 'When would you like to come Mrs Smith?'
Client: 'Tuesday.'
Receptionist: 'We can offer 9.30 a.m. or 10.00 a.m.'
If the client says can you make it later, offer 10.30 or 10.45 and so on – not 3.30 p.m.

This approach will then allow for impulse visits later in the day instead of salons turning potential customers away even though they were not busy earlier.

*Staggered appointment systems*

Staggering appointments is one solution to planning work more efficiently. It will:

(1) avoid 'stop/go' working
(2) increase productivity
(3) distribute support staff evenly
(4) reduce congestion at the backwash
(5) reduce congestion at the reception area
(6) reduce stress

*Example*
One trainee works with two stylists as follows:

| Stylist one | Stylist two |
|---|---|
| 9.00 | 9.15 |
| 9.30 | 9.45 |
| 10.00 | 10.15 |
| 10.45 | 11.00 |

Distribution of appointments makes for smoother use of trainees' or shampooists' time. It helps to avoid congestion at the backwash and reception area.

The purpose of three 30 minute appointments and a 45 minute appointment is to allow for extra services which may have been sold (e.g. colouring or perming), late clients, and slow working hairdressers. Some stylists who are very fast may only need four 30 minute appointments and a 45 minute appointment. Junior stylists, however, usually need two 30 minute appointments and a 45 minute appointment until their speed increases with practice.

The concept of staggered appointments means that two or three stylists work as a team with a trainee or salon assistant to ensure a smooth work flow. This is important for support staff who are often asked to carry out several tasks all at the same time!

### 7.2.2 Operational tasks

There are a number of areas in the running of a salon which, if planned in advance, can make the daily routine more efficient and cost effective and reduce stress levels for staff and clients.

*Duty rotas*

Many salons have duty rotas for trainees to ensure that the daily tasks are completed. Whether the salon has trainees or not – and in the future many will not – the daily tasks need to be completed. These should be split into: a.m. daily tasks, p.m. daily tasks; weekly tasks; monthly tasks.

It is important to ensure that rotas are:

● Fair – jobs are distributed to male and female staff equally (equality means fair distribution of work for both sexes)
● Reasonable tasks, i.e. not being asked to scrub the floor with a toothbrush!
● Achievable, e.g. equipment and cleaning materials are available to complete the task

- Rotated regularly so that some employees do not get all the boring or dirty jobs

*Stock control*

We have already identified in Chapter 2 Understanding money how important it is to control direct costs. Stock control is a key area. The main objectives are to ensure:

- Stock percentages remain constant
- Stock does not run out
- We do not over purchase

This means having systems and standards within our salon to ensure we control stock levels. Who is responsible for stock control and how often is it taken – once a week, fortnightly or monthly? Most major manufacturers will supply salons with stock control forms. One or two staff at most should be responsible for ensuring that the system is kept. The more staff involved in controlling stock, the more mistakes will be made. Stock levels rise for a number of reasons:

- Wastage
- Pilfering
- Purchasing methods

*Wastage* Salons must clearly identify in their training of staff the amount to be measured of:

- Tints
- Bleach/peroxide
- Perm lotion
- Neutraliser
- Shampoo
- Conditioners

What may appear to be small quantities of wasted products accumulates over a 12 month period into a substantial amount of lost product and money.

*Pilfering* Pilfering often occurs in salons because:

- The stock is not secure
- Staff are not allowed stock at cost or free
- There is no staff purchase book
- There is no stock control

Systems for staff purchases ensure that you control stock and monitor how much is being used, particularly by any individual member of staff. (We have all heard of staff with four grandmothers and 20 sisters!)

If you expect staff to wear the products and styles of the salon you must offer products either free or at cost price otherwise you encourage pilfering.

*Purchasing methods* Many salons purchase excessive stock for a number of reasons:

- No stock control
- Smooth talking salesmen
- An attractive incentive scheme
- To obtain higher discounts

With most hair product manufacturers, the larger the order, the higher the discount. This does not mean, however, that you have to purchase a large quantity of one product, e.g. a brand-name perm, but to pledge that over a 12 month period you will spend £x. The higher the total spent the higher the percentage discount. This does not mean that all salons would benefit from a higher discount on products in purely financial terms. Some salons prefer to negotiate 'non-financial' discounts such as promotions, training or marketing expertise (see Chapter 1 on Marketing and promotions for further information).

The key to successful purchasing is always stock control coupled with putting 90 per cent of the salon's purchasing power with one manufacturer who can offer either attractive discounts or, alternatively, business support and expertise.

*Client record cards*

How many clients come through your salon during a week? One hundred, two hundred, five hundred? How many clients will come in next week and the week after that? Can you remember all of their names, where they live, what service was carried out on their hair on their last visit to the salon? You must have some method of recording information about your clients. There are three key reasons for doing this:

(1) Technical information
(2) Personal details
(3) Promotional aid

Obtaining information about your clients prior to the visit helps with planning and organisation because you can:

● Anticipate the client's needs
● Look efficient which creates a good image
● Reduce your own stress levels
● Reduce memory overload

*Technical information* You need some kind of record for perming and colouring to ensure that you know:

(1) how long it was since the client last had a technical service
(2) what products and/or colours were used on her hair

This is essential, not only to trace any potential problems or complaints regarding the service, but also to save time when recommending future technical work.

If you collect information accurately, then it is easy to recommend retail home care products for the client's use in conjunction with perm or colour. You can identify if she is having problems in handling her hair at home and make the appropriate recommendations.

*Personal details* Clients like to feel they are special, particularly if they have been visiting the salon for some time. They expect the salon to know their name, where they live and some information about their personal life such as whether they are married or single, have any children, or what they may do for a living. Information collected in this way helps to build up a picture of a client. It creates a personal relationship with them and makes it easier to sell our services.

*Promotional aid* If you collect information about the type of clients, their age group and the services they have received, then it becomes easier to identify what type of promotional activity would suit the client. It is *always easier* to sell to regular and loyal clients than it is to new clients. It makes promotional activity much more personalised so that you are likely to get a higher response rate than a 'hit and miss' approach. Without collecting information about clients you will find you either forget them or your memory goes into overload.

In conclusion, if you wish operational tasks in the salon to run more smoothly thereby creating a happier working environment, you must ensure you train staff not only *how to make the systems function but why they are important.*

## 7.3 Business planning

Now you have organised yourself and your staff you should have plenty of time to plan your business so that you control it instead of it controlling you! When first opening a hairdressing salon the owner and/or manager tends to be concerned with building a reputation in the locality and making money so that the business continues to exist. After the business has been operating for some years, many salon owners start to ask themselves such questions as:

- Why do I work?
- Is all the hassle worth it?
- Where am I going?
- What do I want?
- How am I going to achieve it?

For most people the key question is 'what do I want?' The answer often eludes us. What options are available? Failure to make time to think and plan for our personal future and the future of the business results in frustration, stagnation and demotivation. This in turn rubs off on the people with whom we may share our lives and those with whom we work. Once we have found the key to what we want by a process of analysis then our energies will be focused and channelled to achieve them.

*What is business planning?*

Business planning is:

(1) Thinking before doing. This means systematically examining alternatives.
(2) Collecting useful information and being aware of the competition in your locality and environment.
(3) Watching competition and 'getting them before they get you'.
(4) Predicting your performance by setting realistic targets and monitoring your actual performance identifying the differences and examining ways of controlling them.
(5) Deciding exactly where the business is going over the next few years and working to achieve this by planning in advance.
(6) Becoming efficient by running your business so that it is economical in operation.

**Fig. 7.1** Stages in business planning.

| | | |
|---|---|---|
| Stage 1 *Plan* | | *Life planning*<br>Who am I?<br>What do I want?<br>Where am I going?<br>What do I want to achieve?<br>What must I do to achieve this? |
| Stage 2 *Measure* | | *Analyse opportunities*<br>How are we doing? Are we good/bad/indifferent?<br>What are the strengths and weaknesses of the<br>    business?<br>What is the competition doing?<br>Who are our customers?<br>What do they want? Do we meet their needs? |
| Stage 3 *Compare* | | *Identify options and alternatives*<br>What are the options available to achieve our<br>    objectives?<br>Expansion? If so, how?<br>New products? Extra staff? Bigger salon?<br>Additional salon?<br>Reduce costs? Increase prices?<br>Retail sales? Motivate staff?<br>Bring in a consultant?<br>More promotion/advertising? Staff training/<br>    development? |
| Stage 4 *Act* | | *Examine alternatives and choose most acceptable in<br>terms of*:<br>● Priority area<br>● Cost effectiveness<br>● Ease of introduction<br>● Quick returns<br>● Most flexible<br><br>This is a personal choice dependent on what you or<br>external 'experts' see to be the priorities. |
| Stage 5 | | *Formulate detailed plans for selected options*<br>● Capital investment and finance<br>● New equipment<br>● New materials<br>● Recruitment and training<br>● Timescale for changes<br>● New systems/procedures/rules<br>● Monitoring/control system for changes<br>● Communicate to relevant staff<br><br>Managing the changes in an effective way is a key<br>part of successful planning<br><br>Produce detailed budgets in terms of:<br>(1) Investments<br>(2) Costs/expenses<br>(3) Revenue/profits<br>(4) Non-quantified benefits<br><br>Communicate these to relevant staff and monitor<br>actual results with those expected/anticipated and<br>act accordingly. |

(7) Controlling the business so that its performance is predictable and manageable, which in turn makes it easier to run.

*What are the benefits for you?*

Planning your business properly will achieve more of the following items than leaving it to chance:

**Fig. 7.2** Business planning – plan of action.

| Types of plans | Questions to ask |
|---|---|
| *Level 1* – Purpose of the business | What is the purpose of the business?<br>Why am I in the business?<br>Why am I a hairdresser? |
| *Level 2* – Major objectives | What purpose does the business serve for me?<br>• An ego trip<br>• A hobby<br>• An income<br>• A way of life<br>What are its objectives?<br>What do I need to do to achieve them? |
| *Level 3* – Strategies | How am I going to achieve the objectives?<br>How do I deal with competition?<br>The environment? Do I ever think about it?<br>(Or wait until it hits me) |
| *Level 4* – Policies or major rules of conduct | What are the rules which will guide my decisions?<br>What are the beliefs I hold which will govern my thinking and structure my decisions? e.g. pricing – I will always be the cheapest/dearest etc. Are these my greatest problems rather than assets? |
| *Level 5* – Procedures and rules | What are the standards and guidelines for staff and management?<br>What are the required standards of behaviour or conduct expected?<br>Are these clear and properly understood? |
| *Level 6* – Programmes or priority projects | What are the current key result areas, projects or activities I am trying to develop in?<br>Have I allocated staff, money and expertise in the right proportion to achieve them? |
| *Level 7* – Budgets | Do I budget ahead?<br>Do I check my actual performance against my budgeted figures?<br>How do I know whether I am:<br>• Successful<br>• Profitable<br>  and/or where I can improve? |

(1) The business will be more successful financially.
(2) Reduced staff problems and miscommunication.
(3) Easier to manage and less hassle.
(4) More time to act – less 'fire-fighting'.
(5) Less 'chopping and changing'.
(6) More control and predictability over performance.
(7) Focus on achieving and rewarding rather than on punishing and scapegoating.
(8) Feel 'on top of the business' instead of 'the business is on top of me'.

In order to achieve business planning we need to look at the five stage process shown in Figure 7.1. Once we have answered these questions then we can consider a plan of action and the questions to ask (Fig. 7.2).

In order to help you to identify the options and alternatives available under Stage 3 in Figure 7.1 we have listed a range of objectives and how these may be achieved in a blow-by-blow approach (Figs 7.3–7.7).

If you have reached this stage in the book then how to plan your business becomes obvious because you now have a systematic approach to help you achieve it. You can begin to understand how the key areas of running a salon all fit together into 'the grand plan' or 'jigsaw'.

**Fig. 7.3** Business planning objectives – how to become rich.

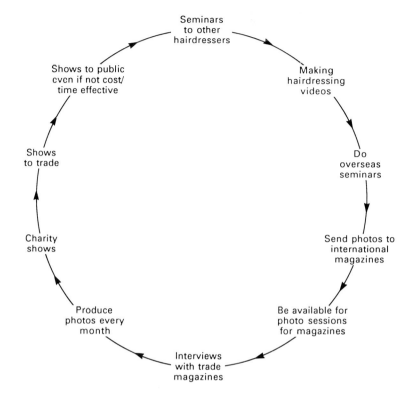

**Fig. 7.4** Business planning objectives – be famous.

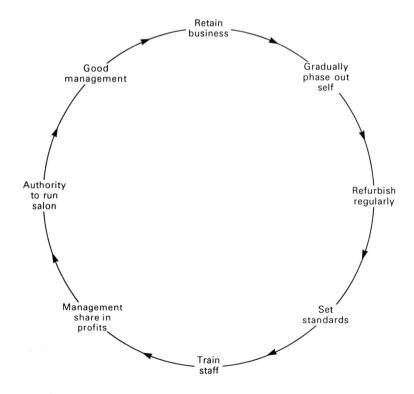

**Fig. 7.5** Business planning objectives – retire/do less work.

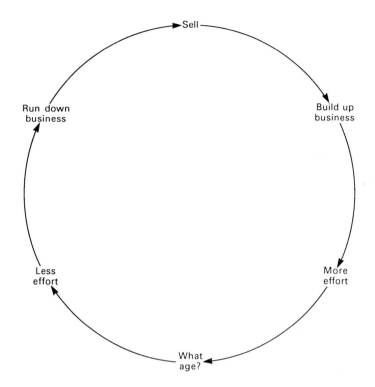

**Fig. 7.6** Business planning objectives – retire.

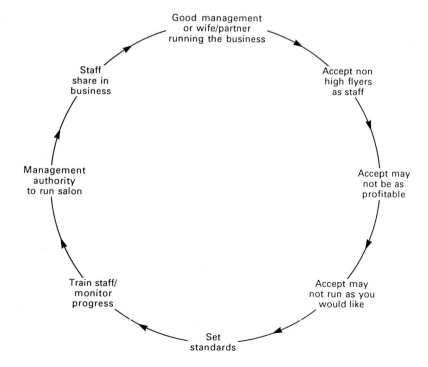

**Fig. 7.7** Business planning objectives – hairdressing as a hobby.

# Chapter Eight
# Managing time and priorities

## 8.1 Planning your time

'If only there were more hours in the day!' 'It is quicker to do the job myself.' 'I don't know where the time has gone.'

All of these statements will sound familiar to the overworked, run-off-his/her-feet manager in the salon. At least, that is often the description the owner or manager would give of himself. The staff probably wonder what the person in question is fussing about as we have all seen salon owners and managers who are 'busy being busy'.

What we are really talking about is the difference between *efficiency* and *effectiveness*.

- Efficiency is doing the job right
- Effectiveness is doing the right job

Effective managers are those who have managed to come to grips with two key issues:

(1) Organising themselves
(2) Organising other people

The two are inter-related because we cannot delegate until we have organised ourselves. What are the keys to an unorganised manager becoming an organised manager?

The first major point is *planning*. Initially, you may have to spend more time to make time, but that is a sensible, positive investment. This means taking control of the time at your disposal and deciding how you want to spend it. But you cannot decide on how you want to spend it until you know where the time has gone now. Then you can examine how you want to use your time and try to move the two things closer together.

Let us look at the ways time is lost:

- Unclear goals
- Lack of planning and organisation
- Unnecessary meetings
- Interruptions and phone calls
- Putting things off
- Too much routine work
- Insufficient delegation
- Lack of self-discipline
- Poor filing/record keeping systems
- Fatigue (lack of rest breaks)
- Long hours
- Physical unfitness
- Pet projects

- Unrealistic timing
- Too many outside interests
- Morale or personal worries

The first stage is to find out how you are spending your time *at present* by keeping some sort of diary or record for a period of at least two weeks but preferably a month. We have drawn up a time recording form which will be easy for you to follow in Fig. 8.1. At the end of each week simply record how much of your time you have spent on various items. We offer a list of

**Fig. 8.1** Time recording form.

**TIME RECORDING FORM**

DAY                    DATE                    NAME

| Time Started | Nature of Activity | Type | Duration | Note Interruptions which occur type/reason/time |
|---|---|---|---|---|
| | | | | |
| | | | | |
| | | | | |
| | | | | |
| | | | | |
| | | | | |
| | | | | |
| | | | | |
| | | | | |
| | | | | |
| | | | | |
| | | | | |
| | | | | |
| | | | | |
| | | | | |
| | | | | |
| | | | | |
| | | | | |

**USEFUL CATEGORIES**

1. Working in Salon (Cutting/Styling)
2. Talking to Staff (Informal)
3. Talking to Customers when not cutting hair (Informal)
4. Dealing with Visitors/Salesmen
5. Ordering and allocating stock
6. Dealing with Correspondence
7. Book-keeping/Accounting etc.
8. Telephone calls—Analyse reason and time spent on the phone. (Personal/Business)
9. Personal Time (Breaks etc)
10. Travelling Time
11. Reading Magazines/Sales Literature etc.
12. Promotional work for salon
13. Promotional work for Manufacturers
14. Unallocated Time

**NOTES FOR USE OF TIME RECORDING FORM**

1. Begin as soon as you begin work or travel to work. Enter time you leave and not arrival time.
2. Each time you begin a **new** activity note the time and note the activity. If you are interrupted while tackling something note the type of interruption (phone call etc) and reason and how long it took to deal with.
3. At the end of the week analyse the sheets and code up the activities according to our scheme (or your own). Add up the total time spent on each category (or class) and also the time spent on all activities and express as percentages of the total.
   e.g. If the total time spent working was 40 hours and you spent 6 hours in the salon cutting/styling this would be:

   6/40 x 100 = **15%** of your time

4. Check that all the percentages add to **100** and you have then completed the weeks analysis. Continue for 4 weeks and then calculate % of time over the whole period. This then is how you currently spend **your** time.

   Also note the number of interruptions on average per week. This forms the first part of **your time** improvement plan.

categories we have found useful but you might like to modify this to suit your own needs.

*Examine the information*

The next phase is more difficult, to examine how you are spending your time and whether it is productive or not.

Look at the unallocated time. This is the time 'lost' – why? Can it be made more useful or cut out completely? *Examine the number of interruptions* – can they be reduced or eliminated? Can someone else answer the phone, take messages and arrange for you to ring back? Can people see you at prearranged times, such as first thing each morning rather than at different times during the day, except in emergencies?

Are you handling jobs following these principles:

• Do one job at a time
• Finish it before going on to the next
• Plan workloads and priorities

Are you clear about your *priorities*? How do you wish to spend your time? Can more routine work be delegated to staff? (Freeing your time and giving them job satisfaction.)

If you are spending too much time on paperwork – are your systems wasting time? Can you find things – have you a proper filing system? Do you have a desk to work at, a comfortable chair, quiet surroundings, a calculator and stationery or is it 'organised chaos'? Is your desk full of old letters, magazines and circulars which you are constantly moving around? Clear your desk of all rubbish – throw it out! Invest in some filing trays – in, out and pending – and use them.

Are you writing where you could phone? Do you use a desk diary for appointments and reminders?

Do you read everything that comes in? If you need it, keep it – if not throw it out.

Do you use a typist? If so, dictation is three times faster than writing things in long hand. It may be worth considering investing in a dictating machine. Do you read information slowly? Perhaps you need a speed reading course?

Now examine in further detail where you spend your time. Is it too much travelling? Would it make sense to live nearer or to travel less often to each shop? A well-run business will run for some of the time without you.

Are you spending too much time cutting hair and not enough time managing? Are you spending too little time talking to staff and solving problems? This can be seen by low morale and general lack of success.

Are you spending enough time *training* staff and maintaining standards through supervision?

Are you spending too much time playing golf? Have you lost touch with your business? This is OK provided you have good quality managers who have been given the responsibility and *authority*, otherwise the business will become neglected.

Figure 8.2 lists possible time wasters, their diagnosis and some suggestions for a cure.

**Fig. 8.2** Time
wasters analysis.

| Time waster | Possible diagnosis | Possible cure |
| --- | --- | --- |
| Unclear priorities/ goals | Inadequate planning. Lack of belief in planning. Busy being busy! | Remember, only politicians redouble their efforts when they have lost sight of their objectives. Write down objectives and agree priorities. |
| Management by crisis | Inadequate forward planning and unrealistic deadlines. Staff bring problems too late. | As above. Allow reasonable time. Think the job through. Allow time for unavoidable interruptions. Be approachable. Encourage staff to bring problems when they occur, not later. |
| Paperwork overload | Too much paperwork. Failure to screen aggressively. Reluctance to tackle paperwork. | Examine systems and improve/streamline if possible. Be selective – throw away things you do not need. Change your attitudes or delegate to someone else who will do the work. |
| Too many interruptions/phone calls | Enjoyment of socialising. Inability to say no. Overkeen to be involved and informed. Lack of self-discipline. Too familiar. Use work to deal with work problems. | Do it elsewhere. Use lunches or after-work drinks. Be realistic – say no. Ensure staff understand their individual responsibility. Only be involved if essential. Manage by exception or delegate. Screen and group calls. Be brief. Decide what you wish to say before you dial. |
| Lack of delegation Too much routine work | Fear of staffs inadequacy. Fear of staffs incompetance. Fear of staff overload. | Assess it correctly. Train where necessary. Delegate properly. Give credit for success. Advise/ correct mistakes, don't punish. Balance up workload so everyone is working hard. |

*Where you want time to go*

Identify active and reactive tasks. This means write a list of all the jobs you have to get done, not just today's but your long term tasks and priorities. It may not be in any order at this stage but just 'brainstorm' the list. It is likely to be a 'mishmash' of large and small tasks, urgent and non urgent, immediate and long term, boring and interesting. Start thinking about the items on the list and try to identify them into *active* and *reactive tasks*.

The active/positive tasks are the ones you must do to achieve the objectives of your job, e.g. make a profit in the salon, train the staff in order that they may function effectively as stylists, promote the salon to attract more clients. The reactive tasks are all the junk that hits you every day and has to be dealt with to keep things running. The danger, and this is the trap that most unorganised managers get into, is that we spend all the available time on reactive tasks – coping with the day to day jobs – and no time on positive tasks.

*Examples of reactive tasks*
(1) Dealing with clients
(2) Supplying clean towels
(3) Tidying the salon
(4) Visiting the wholesaler
(5) Answering the telephone
(6) Client complaints
(7) Staff absenteeism
(8) Broken light bulbs
(9) Burst water pipes

The more you plan your active/positive tasks the shorter will become the list of reactive tasks.

*Schedule your work*

From looking at the list you should now be in a position to schedule your work into the time you have available. To schedule a task you have to know two things:

(1) How long you want to spend on the task. This is determined by how important the task is, for example, promoting the business.
(2) How soon you have to get the task completed. This is determined by how *urgent* the task is. If we do not complete our stock control and order stock from the manufacturer then we will be forced to run down to the wholesaler to purchase stock or to borrow it from the salon across the road!

*Importance* and *urgency* are not the same thing. An urgent task is not necessarily important. It may be urgent but trivial, e.g. do we have fresh milk for clients' coffee, are the shampoo dispensers topped up? Deal with this kind of task straight away. Do not procrastinate and don't spend all morning on discussing the whys and wherefores of the problem. In that way you will leave yourself lots of time for the important tasks.

*Aids to planning your time*

(1) *The Diary* The diary is an important aid to helping you to become more

organised. You can schedule chunks of time in the diary or appointment sheet so you can achieve positive tasks. This means setting time aside for preparing and writing reports, seeing sales reps, having regular meetings with your staff, training staff. You cannot expect that all of these tasks should be completed prior to the salon opening or after the salon closes. Why should you, for example, expect staff meetings to be held at 7.00 p.m. on a Wednesday evening? How about holding them at 8.45–9.30 a.m. one morning? The result would be a more attentive, positive reaction from the staff because the owner or manager has seen that the meeting is sufficiently important to book out the first two appointments on that day.

Use your diary to jog your memory about telephone calls that have to be made. Allocate time twice a day for receiving and making telephone calls instead of constantly excusing yourself from your clients every time a call comes into the salon.

Use your diary to remind yourself of the letters and correspondence which need to be followed through. The diary will help the organised manager to achieve his/her objectives.

(2) *Visual planners* Other devices to help managers are such things as wall charts, year planners and 'bring forward' files. Why search through a mountain of paper when a simple bar or line chart which is updated weekly or monthly can demonstrate sales targets, service targets, training needs and staff holidays? The chart can show you comparisons with previous years and once set up becomes a useful document in managing your business.

Now you have organised your own time you are in a position to organise other people.

## 8.2 Planning your staff's time

Now you have organised yourself how can you organise the team? In Chapter 4 on Managing people we talked about clearly identifying staff's responsibilities and levels of authority and the standards you expect. We discussed that job descriptions must state the minimum standards required and the goals you expect staff to work towards which would, in turn, allow you to manage and motivate your staff further.

Now you have clearly identified where time is spent in your own jobs, can any of these tasks be delegated? Often we hold on to tasks because:

- We enjoy doing them, e.g. photographic work/organising shows
- We can do them more quickly ourselves
- It will be to the standard we expect because we have done it ourselves
- We feel anxious about letting go

Some of the tasks we do ourselves may be very boring and not stretch our own potential but they can be used to stretch and develop others. This will give us more time to spend on the important active tasks.

Delegation does not mean abdication – the buck still stops with the manager/owner even if someone else has been selected to do the actual job. Delegation should be seen like the process of teaching someone to swim or drive a car. When they first start they think they will never get the hang of it and they need constant support, training and *the manager's time* to help them grow and become more confident when performing the tasks.

Unfortunately, some managers believe staff should be thrown in at the deep end to 'sink or swim'. This method of delegation does nothing to help their confidence – some people never swim again! Delegation will ensure that you do not lose overall control – it is the detail which bogs us down so that we fail to perform the key areas of our own jobs.

*Areas for possible delegation*

(1) Appoint a head trainee responsible for trainees
(2) Allocate stylists to be responsible for the day to day training of trainees
(3) Give receptionists responsibility for bookkeeping and paperwork procedures
(4) Allocate a senior stylist or assistant manager to run stock control procedures

The key to delegation is setting the standards you expect from all staff and discussing and agreeing the goals they will work towards.

*Plan of action to delegate*

When deciding to delegate a part of your own job, you may well select a candidate and inform him of the decision. To you this will often mean it should all 'just happen'. But unless your candidate is very able, prepare yourself for a shock. We detail a suggested plan of action:

(1) Decide which tasks to delegate
(2) Decide the staff to whom you will delegate
(3) Brief and train the individual
(4) Inform other people
(5) Be available for discussion/encouragement on key areas of the job
(6) Monitor key areas of the job

In conclusion, by delegating tasks effectively you will gain a considerable amount of time as well as gaining more motivated and interested staff. Staff who, in time, will be able to take more responsibility leaving you time for active, positive tasks. The key points in organising yourself, therefore are:

(1) Make a list
  • positive/active tasks
  • reactive tasks
(2) Establish priorities
  • importance
  • urgency
(3) Schedule your time
  • schedule active tasks
  • allow time for reactive tasks
(4) When organising other people remember to:
  • delegate (which task and who does it)
  • brief people and train them
  • inform others
  • be available for advice
  • check on key points

## Chapter Nine
# The law

## 9.1 Legislation affecting employment of staff

A number of pieces of legislation, dating mainly from 1963, have changed the emphasis with regard to the employer/employee relationship. In consequence, many areas of employing staff are now directly affected by law. The list that directly affects employing staff is outlined below but it is essential that owners and managers refer to the legislation itself, and in cases decided by industrial tribunals, obtain legal advice in relation to their own particular case. The purpose of this summary is to provide a guide as to the areas which need particular attention. We have already detailed in Chapter 3 information regarding contracts of employment and in Chapter 5 detailed the importance of job descriptions, written rules and regulations, grievance procedures and disciplinary procedures which are all part of good employment practice and which considerably reduce the likelihood of an industrial tribunal case.

The legislation directly affecting employment of staff is:

- The Disabled Persons (Employment) Act 1944
- The Contracts of Employment Act 1972
- The Race Relations Act 1976
- The Sex Discrimination Act 1975
- The Employment Protection Act 1978
- The Industrial Training Act 1964
- Employment and Training Act 1973
- The Payment of Wages Act 1960
- The Equal Pay Act 1970
- The Health & Safety at Work Act 1974
- The Redundancy Payments Act 1965

Law, whether it is civil or common law, is a complex issue and just as we have recommended that specialists are consulted for certain aspects of running the business, such is the case with legislation.

One of the most useful reference guides in this area is Croner's *Reference Book for Employers* because it constantly updates the subscriber on any new legislation directly affecting the employment of staff.

### 9.2 Recruitment

In principle, an employer is free to choose whomsoever he/she wishes for employment provided two main categories of legislation are taken into consideration. (See Fig. 9.1.)

(1) Selection on grounds of sex and/or marital status could be held to be discriminatory under the provisions of the Sex Discrimination Act 1975.
(2) Selection on grounds of the race or ethnic origin of the person would be considered unlawful under the provisions of the Race Relations Act 1976.

**Fig. 9.1** Sex and racial discrimination in job adverts.

Sex discrimination (applies if you employ five or more staff)
(1) Avoid words like storeman, salesgirl etc. If these are used make sure the advert clearly offers the job to both sexes.
(2) Make sure the job is not understood as being offered to only one sex.
(3) If the advert uses he, him etc. ensure alternatives are used he/she, him/her and these are consistent throughout.
(4) If pictures are used, show men and women in equal size and prominence *or* a disclaimer (equal opportunities) is needed.

Racial discrimination
(1) Job adverts must not discriminate on racial grounds, i.e. colour, race, nationality, citizenship, ethnic or national origins.

A fine of up to £400 in either case is possible.

In short do not specify: sex, marital status, colour, race or nationality in adverts.

## 9.3 Servicing the employment

The employer must perform certain duties imposed by legislation as follows:
(1) Payment and amount of wages governed by the Payment of Wages Act 1960 and Equal Pay Act 1970
(2) Health and safety of employees whilst employed or *on the employer's premises* affected by the Health and Safety at Work Act 1974
(3) Maternity leave affected by the Employment Protection Act 1978 which gives the pregnant employee four rights:

- the right to time off for ante-natal care
- the right not to be dismissed if the employee has accumulated two years' continuous employment by the beginning of the 11th week before the expected date of the birth
- the right to maternity pay
- the right to return to work within the same position or similar position, if the employee has stated in writing that she intends to do so. The pregnant employee will have up to 29 weeks leave after the date of confinement provided she notifies her employer in writing at least 21 days in advance of her intention to return to work.

For further information regarding this Act, read the Act itself, Croner's *Reference Guide* or contact the DHSS.
For salons employing five staff or less maternity leave does not apply.

## 9.4 Health and Safety at Work Act 1974

There is much legislation regulating health and safety at work. The legislation falls into two categories:

(1) That which is general laying down broad outlines
(2) That which is specific and detailed applying to particular types of premises

The Health and Safety Executive produce a number of free leaflets and Codes of Practice and we have found them particularly helpful in clarifying how to apply this law to hairdressing salons.

It is the duty of every employer, as far as is reasonably practicable, to ensure the health, safety and welfare at work of all staff. This includes, in particular, the following:

- Maintenance of equipment which should be safe and without risk to health, e.g. sterilisers, mixing of chemicals
- Safety in connection with the use, handling, storage and transporting of articles, substances (products) and equipment
- Provision of information and training and supervision to ensure that employees understand health and safety at work
- Provision of access and exits from the place of work which are safe and without risk
- Provision of adequate facilities and arrangements for staff's welfare at work (staff rooms!)

Again, we would strongly recommend that the Health and Safety Executive and Croner's *Reference Guide* are consulted. We have already suggested in Chapter 5 areas which rules should cover and these have incorporated the requirements of the Health and Safety at Work Act.

# Chapter Ten
# The future of the industry

One of the advantages of being a consultant is being able to observe the industry from a wider perspective, whether from the viewpoint of the single salon owner, mobile hairdressers, multi-site salons, franchise organisations, hair product manufacturers or managing agencies. As we move towards the next century, the industry will be forced by market and economic factors to change its approach and attitude if owners/managers wish to make a good living from their businesses.

*Threats/opportunities facing the industry*

- An ageing population
- Franchising
- Shortage of young people
- Home hairdressing
- Skill shortage – stylists/managers/trainers
- 1992

## 10.1 An ageing population

By the year 2000 half the population in the UK will be 40 or over – by the year 2040, 80 per cent of the population will be pensioners (source: OECD, Henley Forecasting Centre)! This raises a number of issues:

*Ageing clients*

When we begin to get older we are looking for a range of sevices with a different emphasis. Often, the older we get and the more experience we have of life, the more discerning we are in terms of what we expect in return for our custom. Until we have a fixed income we may not be price conscious but will certainly expect value for money.

Ask anyone over 35 who visits a hairdressing salon what they expect from their hairdresser:

- Personalised service
- High standards of cleanliness
- Quiet background music
- Convenience – e.g. parking facilities or for the hairdresser to visit them
- Hairdressing/technical services to make him/her younger and desirable
- Hair care advice
- Selection of refreshments (not just tea or coffee)
- Hours to suit the client
- Staff who understand how it feels to be older

In a recent market survey carried out by major manufacturers the typical profile of a hairdresser showed 'an age of 24', 'stays in the industry for five years', 'reads the Daily Mail' and 'shops at Next'! We can see how this can instantly create a communication barrier!

*Ageing hairdressers*

Where do all the old hairdressers go? There has always been a fear among many hairdressers of the thought of getting old, but in fact, with an ageing population, older stylists will come into their own. Older stylists for older clients – so they are able to communicate and understand the client's needs. Where does this leave the present day practice of employing young people as trainees in hairdressing?

There is already a shortage of young people in the industry which will continue through the 1990s. In 1987 there were 27 000 school leavers, half of them employed by just 20 large companies. The rest were fought over by all the remainder of the service sector. ·

Why do we bother to compete? Why not be more selective about the employment of trainees by learning recruitment/selection skills, training them intensely during the day over a 12/18 month period instead of the traditional 2/3 years and paying them a realistic salary whilst training?

The remainder of the hairdressing and support staff could be employed from two other sources:

(1) Women returners who may have previously been hairdressers, now needing refresher courses.
(2) Women returners who have not previously been hairdressers but who could be trained as either hairdressers or salon assistants.

This would meet the needs of an ageing population/clientele. They would be able to understand and communicate with their clients because they will know how it feels to be older and what clients will expect. What prevents this happening?

(1) Attitudes/resistance to change
(2) Low pay

The apprenticeship and YTS scheme have created a false market for a number of years whereby we have paid staff slave-labour wages on the pretext that we cannot afford an alternative. This is rubbish! If owners and managers spent more of their time in running their salons as businesses and developed their skills to be more successful and profitable they would not need to worry about the shortage of school leavers.

*New skills needed by owners/managers*

(1) Recruitment/selection skills
(2) Understanding money and pricing strategy
(3) Planning and organisational skills
(4) Man-management skills
(5) Training to train
(6) Promotions/marketing
(7) Computerisation

Owners and managers who do not take this path to solve their problems will need to take alternative action such as:

(1) home hairdressing, or
(2) franchising

In 1989 approximately 40 per cent of hairdressers were either employed as home hairdressers or self-employed. It is our prediction based upon these marketing and economic factors that this figure will continue to increase throughout the 1990s to 60 per cent if we do not attract or harness this growing sector of the industry. Not all home hairdressers are unprofessional. They do meet a demand. The market research surveys we have carried out show that clients, particularly those with families, want the convenience of home hairdressers. These clients are saying we do not meet their needs. Hairdressers have tended to discourage children from visiting salons – but this action discourages the parents too. In the mid-1980s there was an increase in the birthrate – children have become a 'fashionable accessory' (although this is not necessarily the authors' view) and we need to rethink our approach to the family as a 'one client unit' in terms of service and pricing strategy.

## 10.2 Franchising

During the 1980s a number of companies developed into the franchising market, each with their own strengths and weaknesses. These companies were the pioneers in this industry and as new companies move into franchising they will learn from the mistakes of others.

The strengths of franchise companies are often the weaknesses of many small salons who need to compete with them to survive. Small businesses lack resources – this means they have to do all their own paperwork, training, recruitment and stock control as well as come up with promotional and marketing ideas. Work like this is usually carried out at weekends or in the evenings and experience is often gained through costly mistakes.

This is where franchising comes into its own. Franchising companies are able to offer their franchisees organised promotional back-up, both locally and nationally, to attract clients. A franchise salon uses the reputation of a large company and offers support systems and controls to help a franchisee become successful more quickly. Franchise companies may offer:

- Induction training
- Hairdressing training
- Management and career development training
- Paperwork systems
- Discounts on stock
- PR/promotional back-up

These are the franchise companies to join – but at what cost? What kind of percentage should franchisees be paying for this range of services? It could be anything from 5–10 per cent depending upon what the franchisee gets in return. When thinking of this market it always pays to shop around and compare as much as possible like with like.

How does the small salon owner who wants to 'go it alone' compete with a large, well organised company? The answer is to beat them at their own game. This means becoming organised, delegating to staff, setting up training and career structures and setting standards of what you expect from them. In fact, the salon owner or manager who reads this book will have the clues as to how to make these things happen for them.

## 10.3  Home hairdressers

Why does a stylist become a home hairdresser? Some of the reasons for this are:

- Increased flexibility in working hours
- Less responsibility
- More money
- No salon politics

In the previous section we suggested that we need to attract this growing sector of the industry. There are many disadvantages to being a home hairdresser, as a number discover after two to three years, which is the average time that home hairdressers stay out there on their own. Many of them would be interested in working within a structured organisation where there is stimulus and creativity and greater job security. But the rewards must be great too. We have another reason for suggesting we consider harnessing this market and using home hairdressers as part-time staff.

Professor Charles Handy, who is visiting Professor at the London Business School, predicted in his book *The Age of Unreason* (Century Hutchinson) that part-time work will be normal by the end of this decade. He put forward his 'shamrock' theory whereby the work force would be made up of three types of workers.

At the moment there are 24 million people employed in this country. Some 16 million of them are full time, meaning that one-third of the entire population work part time. He predicted that within the next ten years half of the entire working population would be employed on a part-time basis. He suggested that employment trends over the next few years will change so dramatically that the working population will fall into three sectors:

(1) A core of highly paid professionals
(2) A flexible workforce
(3) A contractual fringe

He considered that the core of highly paid professionals would enjoy high pay, long term contracts, good benefits and expensive company cars. The flexible workforce would be employed, he suggested, on an annual hours agreement so that they worked to meet the demands of the business and to fit in with their own domestic commitments. This type of workforce will be ideal for salons who open 12 hours a day, seven days a week, and for those busy periods at Christmas and Easter. As some two-thirds of the country is now developing towards the service industry as opposed to manufacturing, which requires people to work a wider variety of hours and days of the week, how can the hairdressing industry meet this change in people's working patterns? The answer is that hairdressing salons will have to respond by opening longer hours and more days of the week.

An alternative approach to looking at the trend of home hairdressing is to use it as an opportunity – to expand your business into the home hairdressing market. For example, why is it that there is a home hairdressing market at all? Women who have children and domestic commitments often find that salon hours from 9 a.m.–6 p.m. are not compatible with feeding, shopping, delivering and collecting children from school. Yet, many of these women are experienced workers who would work extremely hard at the salon but who have other priorities in their lives. If we do not consider attracting these people back into the fold then we create another rod for our own backs.

# Appendix
# Sources of information

## Marketing and promotions

Small Firms Advisory Bureau.
Institute of Marketing.
Institute of Practitioners in Advertising.
British Institute of Management.
Market Research Society.
British Direct Mail Marketing Association.
Institute of Public Relations.
Institute of Sales Promotion.
Advertising Standards Authority.
Winner, Paul, *Effective PR Management – A Guide to Corporate Survival* Kogan Page.

## Understanding money

Murray, J., *Success in Bookkeeping for Small Businesses* Whitehead.
    *Success in Principles of Accounting* Whitehead.
    *Insight into Management Accounting* Penguin.
    *Managing Your Business* Eaglemoss.
Fisher, *Controlling Labour Costs* Kogan Page.
Pizzey, *Accounting and Finance* Holt.
Mogano, *How to Start and Run Your Own Business* Graham and Trotman.
ISM, *Salon Management Fax Guide – Financial Section* (specially written for the hairdressing industry).

*Potential sources of finance*

All major banks and smaller banks.
Building Societies.
Insurance Companies.
3i Investment in Industry.
ICFC Industrial and Commercial Finance Corporation, 7 Copthall Avenue, London, EC23 7DD.
European Business Development.
Small Business Capital Fund.
Small Firms Information Service (contact local branch).

## Finding staff and keeping them

Armstrong, M., *Handbook of Personnel Management Practice* Kogan Page.
Equal Opportunities Commission (Sex/Race Discrimination), Quay Street, Manchester, M3 3HN.

Local colleges or polytechnics.
Institute of Personnel Management, Camp Road, Wimbledon, SW19 4UW.
British Institute of Management, Management House, Parker Street, London, WC2.
Miller, K., *Psychological Testing in Personnel Assessment* Gower.
ISM, Woodlands, 9 York Road, Malton, North Yorkshire, YO17 0AX.

## Managing and motivating staff

Handy, C., *Understanding Organisations* Penguin.
Vroom and Deci, *Management and Motivation* Penguin.
Armstrong, M., *Salary Administration* Kogan Page.
Lupton, T. and Gowler, D., *Selecting a Wage Payment System* Kogan Page.
Armstrong, *Handbook of Personnel Management Practice* Kogan Page.
Warr, P.B., *Psychology at Work* Penguin.
Warwick Institute for Employment Research.
Kanter, P., *The Change Masters* BBC Video and Unwin Paperbacks.
Handy, C. *The Age of Unreason* Century Hutchinson.

# Index

acquiring a business, 45
administrative training, 82
advertising
    employment and law, 159
    job vacancies, 61
ageing
    hairdressers, 163
    population, 162
analysing
    the job, 49
    the person, recruitment, 59
analysis of training needs, 129
applying theory, marketing, 24
appointment systems, 142
attracting potential staff, 61

behaviour, 113
    leadership styles, 115
bonus schemes, 110
business, how is the salon doing?, 29
business planning, 146

capital raising, 27
cash flow forecast, 30
client
    information, 24, 145
    satisfaction, 5
    satisfaction survey, 6
clients
    needs in the future, 7
    what do they want?, 6
    who are they?, 6
communication, 89
    training, 80
competitors analysis, 17
conditions of employment, 76
contribution to gross profit, 35
costs
    controlling, 40, 42
    stock, 143
customer service training, 81

descriptions, job, 51
direct costs, controlling, 40

discipline
    the interview, 125
    the process, 124
    what is it?, 119

employment forms, application for, 64
employment law, 159
employment, terms and conditions, 76
evaluating training, 139
expenses, controlling, 42

finance, raising it, 27
finding staff, 48
franchising, 164
future of the industry, 162

Goldthorpe, motivational theory, 102

hair product manufacturers, 167
handling staff problems, 119
health and safety at work, 160
Herzberg, motivational theory, 100
home hairdressers, 165

identifying training needs, 129
image
    advertising, 14
    pricing and its effect, 21
    selecting an, 11
increasing turnover/sales, 34, 37
induction training, 78
information on
    clients, 24
    competitors, 24
    products, 24
    staff, 24
initial screening, recruitment, 66
integration of new staff, 77
interviews, job selection, 67

job analysis, 49
job descriptions, 51
job vacancies, writing advertisements, 61

keeping staff, 48

law, 159
leadership styles, 115
legislation affecting employment, 159
listening skills, 94

management training, 82
managers, their role, 84
managing
    people, 84
    time, 152
manufacturers
    help from, 14, 24, 29, 40, 80, 144
    the future, 167
market mix, 10
market segmentation, 8
marketing, 1
Maslow, motivational theory, 99
Mayo, motivational theory, 99
McClelland, motivational theory, 101
medical examinations, 74
money, understanding, 27
motivation, 96
    practical application, 103
    theory, 98

needs, analysis of training, 129

objectives, training, 131
organisational skills, 140
organising
    own time, 152
    staff's time, 157

pay schemes, designing, 108
people, managing, 84
person specifications, 59
planning
    business, 146
    the salon, 140
    time, 152
    training programmes, 132
    the work, 142
pricing, 17
problems, staff, 119
productivity
    salon layout, 141
    staff, 37
products, image of, 14
promotional ideas, 25
promotions, 1

questionnaires
    client satisfaction, 5

competitors, 6
motivation, 97
questioning techniques, recruitment, 69

raising finance, 27
recruitment, 48
references, recruitment, 73
revenue increasing, 37
rotas, duty, 143
rules, designing, 121

sales, increasing revenue, 37
school leavers, decline of, 79
screening, potential candidates, 66
segmentation market, 7
selecting an image, 11
selection, methods of, 72
selling a business, 45
services, training 81
setting standards
    appearance, 56
    behaviour, 57
    hairdressing, 56
    performance, 56
    service, 57
skill shortage
    managers, 163
    stylists, 166
staff, finding them, 48
stock control, 144
strategies, interviewing discipline, 126
styles, leadership, 115
stylists, analysis form, 4
systems, training, 82

Taylor, motivational theory, 98
terms and conditions of employment, 76
time
    managing, 152
    planning your own, 152
    planning your staffs, 157
training, 129
    aids, 135
    analysis of training needs, 129
    admin/systems, 82
    communication skills, 80
    defining objectives, 131
    evaluation, 139
    management, 82
    programmes, 132
    service skills, 81
    technical, 79
    techniques, 133

trial periods, 78

understanding money, 27

visual aids, training, 135
Vroom, motivational theory, 101

women returners, 163